The Sales
Closing Book

SellingPower
Open More Doors. Close More Sales.

The Sales Closing Book

Field-Tested Closes for Every Selling Situation

Gerhard Gschwandtner

McGRAW-HILL

New York   Chicago   San Francisco   Lisbon   London   Madrid   Mexico City
Milan   New Delhi   San Juan   Seoul   Singapore   Sydney   Toronto

The **McGraw-Hill** Companies

1 2 3 4 5 6 7 8 9 0   DOC/DOC   0 9 8 7 6

ISBN-13: P/N 978-0-07-147601-0 of set
            978-0-07-147860-1

ISBN-10: P/N 0-07-147601-6 of set
            0-07-147860-4

McGraw-Hill books are available at special quantity discounts to use as
premiums and sales promotions, or for use in corporate training programs.
For more information, please write to the Director of Special Sales,
Professional Publishing, McGraw-Hill, Two Penn Plaza, New York, NY
10121-2298. Or contact your local bookstore.

Library of Congress Cataloging-in-Publication Data
Gschwandtner, Gerhard.
     The sales closing book / by Gerhard Gschwandtner.
        p. cm.
     ISBN 0-07-147860-4 (alk. paper)
     1. Selling.   I. Title

     HF5438.25.G7835 2007
     658.85--dc22   2006046654

Contents

CONTENTS

Introduction

The Sales Closing Book

"The close is the keystone to your success."

> **Life is too short to learn only from experience.**

The information in this book has been collected in primarily three ways: (1) from interviews with more than 200 master sales closers during the past 15 years, (2) from researching more than 2,000 books on selling in the Library of Congress in Washington, D.C., and (3) from my own personal selling experiences over the past 25 years.

Just about any salesperson can find a new prospect, open a sale, or take an order. However, it takes a trained, motivated, and skilled professional to close the sale.

The inability to close a sale always costs more than the profit lost from the order. A lost order can hurt our pride or injure our self-esteem. In addition, losing a sale tends to throw a monkey wrench into our dreams of success.

A lost sale unleashes a silent outcry for better closing techniques. Deep down inside we speculate on what we could have achieved with better skills. *The Sales Closing Book* has been developed to act as a personal guide and coach for your future sales success.

Five Ways to Get the Most Out of This Book

1. Write your current closing ratio on page xiii. Each time you study this book, write the actual time you spent with this book in the study log. Update your closing ratio every three months and monitor your closing progress.

2. Try a new close every week. At the end of the year you will have mastered 52 new ways to close the sale.

3. Videotape your closing skills and review the tape with your colleagues.

4. Practice the closes in this book with your personal audio recorder. As the owner of this book, you are legally entitled to record the closing techniques in this book for your own personal use. (U.S. copyright laws prohibit you from using your recording for commercial purposes.) This exercise is especially important for practicing story closes and analogy closes.

5. Add new closes to your book in the spaces provided.

Chart Your Closing Progress

Complete this chart before you begin reading this book.

My name: _____

My current closing ratio: _____

Current date: _____

Complete the following information after each reading.

Date of second reading: _____

Closing ratio at time of second reading: _____

Date of third reading: _____

Closing ratio at time of third reading: _____

Date of fourth reading: _____

Closing ratio at time of fourth reading: _____

Date of fifth reading: _____

Closing ratio at time of fifth reading: _____

Date of sixth reading: _____

Closing ratio at time of sixth reading: _____

Date of seventh reading: _____

Closing ratio at time of seventh reading: _____

Date of eighth reading: _____

Closing ratio at time of eighth reading: _____

Date of ninth reading: _____

Closing ratio at time of ninth reading: _____

Date of tenth reading: _____

Closing ratio at time of tenth reading: _____

CHAPTER

1

The Trial Close

Take your prospect's temperature.

- Successful Trial Closes Following Signs of Approval
- Successful Trial Closes after Stating Customer Benefits
- Successful Trial Closes after Customer Objections
- General Trial Closing Questions

Taking Your Prospect's Temperature

The purpose of a trial close is to assess your prospect's readiness to buy your product or service.

You may remember from your childhood how your mom or dad took a toothpick and poked a cake in the oven to find out if it was ready. If the toothpick came out clean, the cake came out of the oven. If there was any dough sticking on the toothpick, you had to wait a little longer for your cake.

In selling we use trial closes to check if the prospect is ready to buy. After a series of positive answers to our trial closes, we know that the prospect is ready for the final closing question.

Trial closes offer three distinct advantages. First, they minimize the risk of your customer saying no. Second, they help you smoke out hidden objections. Third, they will conceal your closing efforts. You will be able to make other people feel that your idea was really theirs.

Overcoming Your Closing Fears

Modern sales psychology tells us that closing takes courage. The closing process is the resolution of an internal struggle between the need for ego protection and the need for ego gratification. On one hand, we want the sale (ego gratification); on the other hand, we want to protect ourselves against being turned down (ego protection).

Salespeople who don't want to risk having their egos bruised tend to put off asking for the order. They know that as long as they don't ask for the order, they can't get hurt. The problem with this approach is that buyers will quickly sense a salesperson's fear of closing and come up with more reasons for not buying.

Salespeople who lack courage tend to get caught in a vicious cycle. Their fear of closing will actually increase the prospect's fear of buying. Prospects will be tempted to think, "If he is not confident enough to ask me for the order, I have no reason to be confident in his proposition."

> **Fear is the terror inspired by ignorance.**
> **—Edgar Russell**

The inability to overcome fear is the root cause of failure in selling. The best way to gain the necessary courage to ask for the order with the lowest risk of hearing a no is the trial close.

When Should You Use Trial Closes?

1. *When you see signs of approval from your prospect.* Note the positive body language, approving noises, broad smile, subtle hand movement stroking the product, relaxed posture, and so on.

2. *After you state a major customer benefit.* Add trial closes to your presentation after you have explained the cost savings, after you have proven the increased productivity, after you have shown your testimonial letters, and after you have completed your product demonstration.

3. *After you answer an objection.* Respond to the price objection and follow up with a trial close. Handle the "I have to think about it" objection and use a trial close.

Successful Trial Closes Following Signs of Approval

1.   I can see that you have a preference for this model. Is that what you had in mind?

2.   I noticed your smile when you looked at this brochure. Don't you think that this would look great in your office?

3.   Do I assume correctly that if you were to choose a new machine, you would want to get the faster one?

4.   You seem to be happy with the features of this color copier. Can you imagine how your productivity will go up if you get this one?

5. I get the impression that this car fits your driving style better than you expected. Am I reading you correctly?

6. I noticed that you were taking pictures of the trees lining the driveway. Don't you think that the approach alone makes this property a very special investment?

7. I can see that you are excited about this product. On a scale of 1 to 10, how do you feel it will fit your needs?

8. Something tells me that you are falling in love with this beautiful car. Am I right?

9. I have a hunch that you like the money-saving features of this instrument. Did I guess that right?

10. _____

_____

_____

11. _____

_____

_____

Successful Trial Closes after Stating Customer Benefits

1. You will be pleased to know that we will protect your investment in two ways. First, you have our factory warranty, which as you know covers parts and labor for five years. But more important, our company will give you a free loaner should we be unable to fix your problem within 24 hours. Is it important to you to have this type of security in doing business with us?

2. This model has an automatic collating feature that will save you about five hours per week in clerical time. Don't you think that this savings alone would justify the investment in a more productive machine?

3. Many of our customers have used this kind of cookware for over 40 years. Don't you think it makes good economic sense to get something that will save you money and will pay for itself, rather than buying a new set every 5 years?

4. Now that I have demonstrated the top three features of this machine, which one do you feel will help you the most in your particular situation?

5. I think that this model would suit you best. Would you want me to call the warehouse to find out if we have any left?

6. _____

_____

_____

7. _____

_____

_____

Successful Trial Closes after Customer Objections

1. Just suppose for a moment that price would be no problem. Would you be happy with this product?

2. Let's assume for a moment that I could show you a way you could afford this product without draining your cash reserves. Would you consider buying it?

3. The only question you need to ask yourself is: Do I want to pay a little more than I figured now, or am I willing to pay a much higher price later?

4. I understand your concerns about the higher price. Isn't it interesting that the more we want something, the more we find that other people want the same thing. Unfortunately that's the reason why we've had this price increase, but honestly, it hasn't stopped people from wanting it even more. That's really very positive because your resale value is going up too. Don't you think that you'd rather invest in something that goes up in value?

5. I understand that you want to wait. It's always good to weigh the pros and cons of such an important decision. The only question you need to ask yourself is: How much does it cost me per day, per week, and per month not to have a reliable and safe machine in my plant?

6. _____

_____

_____

7. _____

_____

_____

General Trial Closing Questions

1. How are we doing so far?

2. Are we on the right track with this proposal?

3. Is this demonstration progressing according to your expectations?

4. Is this the type of comfort and safety that you had mind?

5. Are you asking yourself: When could I get one delivered?

6. Are you asking yourself: How could I be productive without it?

7. Don't you feel that this is the best model on the market?

8. Don't you think that after you have seen this, you won't want to look at anything else?

9. Doesn't this feature alone justify the investment?

10. Can't you just see your boss giving you a raise when you show him how much this will increase production?

11. Just think about the money you will save day after day. Isn't this a good enough reason to have one delivered next week?

> **The best way to work up the courage to ask for the order is the trial close.**

12. What do we need to do to get you started?

13. _____

_____

_____

14. _____

_____

_____

CHAPTER 2

The Story Close

Always lead your prospect, never push.

- A Humorous Story to Sell the Customer on Paying Cash
- A Short Story to Relax a Worried Prospect
- The Acres-of-Diamonds Story to Sell a Special Opportunity
- A Humorous Story to Avoid Lowering Your Price
- The Satisfied-Customer Story to Reassure Your Prospect
- The Satisfied-Customer Story to Justify the Price
- Develop Stories That Close Sales

What We Can Learn from Great Storytellers

Good storytellers are good sales closers. They know how to captivate the imagination of their prospects and let the story illustrate the selling point in a most elegant and persuasive way.

A brief story always adds value to the relationship.

The process of storytelling is mysterious and little understood by amateur salespeople. They often feel that telling a story may not be perceived as businesslike. Or they underestimate the tremendous psychological powers of a good story.

Ronald Reagan's Disarming Stories

Former President Ronald Reagan, the son of a shoe salesman, used many short stories to illustrate his political selling points. Former House Speaker Tip O'Neill was once quoted as saying about Reagan: "He's always got a disarming story. I don't know where he gets them, but he's always got them. He calls up: 'Tip, you and I are political enemies only until six o'clock. It's four o'clock now; can we pretend it's six o'clock?' How can you dislike a guy like that?"

Tip O'Neill's comment illustrates how a good storyteller can relax the opponent's defenses. Ronald Reagan's closing technique was a simple two-step process: First disarm, then close.

A Country Lawyer's Famous Story

Robert F. Kennedy wrote in his book *The Enemy Within* about another great American storyteller, Senator Sam J. Ervin, Jr.: "I heard Senator Ervin on several occasions destroy a witness by telling an appropriate story which made the point better than an hour-long speech or a day of questioning."

> **What can you offer in exchange for your prospect's time?**

During the McCarthy hearings, Senator Ervin influenced the opinions of the entire Senate committee and the nation with this humorous story:

> A young lawyer went to an old lawyer for advice as to how to try a lawsuit. The old lawyer said, "If the evidence is against you, talk about the law. If the law is against you, talk about the evidence."

> The young lawyer asked, "But what do you do when both the law and the evidence are against you?"

> "In that case," said the old lawyer, "give somebody hell. That will distract the attention of the judge and the jury from the weakness of your case."

Although Senator Ervin never said that McCarthy had a weak case, his story drove his point home in an unforgettable way.

Some psychologists claim that we tend to reexperience a sense of childhood wonder and amazement when we listen to a story. The astute storyteller uses this little-known fact to sell his or her ideas.

The Three Benefits of a Good Story

1. *Stories relax.* Your story is bound to change the emotional climate of the conversation in a pleasant way. The more relaxed your prospect becomes, the more agreeable he will be to your proposal.

2. *Stories captivate.* Your story will recapture your prospect's full attention. Her mind will focus only on your story, and chances are that she will forget her preoccupations about the purchase.

3. *Stories drive home closing points.* The characters in your story will do the selling for you. All you have to do is set the stage, unfold the plot, and let the characters close the deal for you.

> **Closing is an art. The greatest art conceals art.**

A Humorous Story to Sell the Customer on Paying Cash

A sign in a restaurant said: "You want credit—I say 'no' . . . you get sore. You want credit—I say 'yes' . . . you don't pay, I get sore. Better you get sore than I get sore."

Mr. Brown, this is a very special sale, and we want to make sure that nobody gets sore and everybody's happy. Don't you agree?

A Short Story to Relax a Worried Prospect

I understand that you are a little concerned about this purchase. You don't need to worry because our informal research shows that almost 100 percent of our customers do not lose more than two nights' worth of sleep when they buy from us. [Smile.]

Were you aware of that?

[Wait for reply.]

It's true. The first night they worry is usually before they buy because they worry about making the right decision. But amazingly, they also lose sleep the night after they've bought because then they worry why we've sold such a great value at such a low price. [Smile.]

I am really confident that you will be totally satisfied with this product, or we'll gladly refund your money within 30 days.

Fair enough?

The Acres-of-Diamonds Story to Sell a Special Opportunity

Mr. Smith, have you ever heard the story called "Acres of Diamonds"? You see, there was this fellow who sold his farm and traveled all over the world looking for diamonds. He searched and searched, but he couldn't find any. Finally he came back home, old and broke, to find that the biggest diamond mine in the world had been discovered right on his farm, and the man he had sold his farm to had become one of the richest men in the world.

Mr. Smith, the opportunity we have been discussing is like the farm in that story. Today you can't see the diamonds—you see only the farm. But once you start digging a little bit, you will find that you don't need to work hard until you are old and broke, but you can work smarter and make a lot more money in the process.

Don't give up on your right to take advantage of this opportunity. Let's roll up our sleeves now and get the ball rolling.

Adapt this story to your selling situation:

_____

_____

_____

A Humorous Story to Avoid Lowering Your Price

This reminds me of a story from the jewelry business. A wholesale jeweler wanted to get $12,000 for a beautiful diamond ring, but her customer, a shrewd retailer like you, wanted to pay only $10,000.

Finally, the wholesaler sent the ring insured with a letter stating that the final price was $12,000—take it or leave it. If he didn't want the ring at that fair price, he was to simply send back the ring.

Ten days later, the wholesaler received a package with a check for $10,000 and a note saying: "Here is my check for your ring. If you accept it, please return the package without opening it. But if you still insist on $12,000, please return my check for $10,000 and keep the package."

The wholesaler got angry because she needed to cover her costs and get the full price. She decided to open the package and put the ring back into her inventory. But the package contained only a little note and a check. The note said: "Don't get excited— here is the rest of your money." The check was written for $2,000.

I thought you would enjoy this story because I know that you'd love to get away with paying less, but I need to cover my costs and at the same time help you understand that our price is fair. So please write the check for the full amount.

Customize the story by using a dollar amount that is equal to the discount your customer has asked for.

The Satisfied-Customer Story to Reassure Your Prospect

Mrs. Brown, I am glad you mentioned that. You will be pleased to hear that many of our customers have used this product more than eight years without major problems.

You may know Mr. Harvey Kirshner, the chairman of Interstate, Inc. He was convinced that our machine would not make it through the first week on the job. [Pause.]

That was three years ago. He has since bought seven more. He told me just last month that buying our product was the smartest decision he ever made.

I know that you'll be glad you made the decision to go with us. Shall we go over the details?

Develop a true, satisfied-customer story to reassure your prospects:

_____

_____

_____

The Satisfied-Customer Story to Justify the Price

Mr. Smith, I am glad you mention price because that's exactly why you should buy from us. Last week I visited with Ms. Biddle. You probably know her from the Chamber of Commerce meetings, don't you? [Wait for reply.]

Well, when Ms. Biddle sold her machine, she got 80 percent of her original investment back. She had used the machine for over three very productive years. [Pause.]

You see, when you figure the total value of this machine, you need to deduct the resale value. Since our resale value is expected to be much higher, just as in Ms. Biddle's case, your total cost will be much lower.

I assume that you are looking for a machine that maintains its value for a long time. Am I correct? [Wait for reply.]

I am glad we agree. [Smile.] When would you need delivery?

Develop a true story to justify the price:

_____

_____

_____

Develop Stories That Close Sales

The most effective stories that sell are unembellished, satisfied-customer stories. They can help reassure your prospect, prove the value of your service, enhance the quality of your product, or lead to a larger order than you expected.

When you collect success stories, get every single detail you can. Describe the customer's struggle before he or she bought your product. Explain what happened when your product was first used. Record your customer's positive comments.

Write out the details of your story, and be sure it is short, clear, and interesting.

Rehearse telling your story with family members or friends before you use it to close your sale.

Write your sales closing stories on 3- by 5-inch cards. Develop at least five good sales closing stories.

Action idea: Interview satisfied clients and record the interviews. Get their permission to play back their comments to new prospects. (Ask them to sign a release form—check with your legal department on how to obtain one.) Bring your interviews to a professional audio recording studio. Ask the sound engineer to edit your satisfied-customer interviews into a series of short stories and splice them together so you'll end up with a single audio file. Let your cassette tell the story of your success.

CHAPTER 3

The "Yes-Set" Close

Put your prospect in the "yes" mindset.

- Tested and Proven "Yes-Set" Closes

How You Can Win with the "Yes-Set" Close

The goal of the "yes-set" close is to establish an atmosphere of agreement with the prospect before asking for the order.

This powerful close consists of asking a series of questions that will lead to a predictable "yes" response.

Master sales closers know that if their prospects get into a mental pattern of saying "yes" to a series of minor questions, it will become very difficult for them to say "no" to the final closing question.

Here is a typical example:

Salesperson: Do you like the e-mail features that come with this computer?

Customer: Yes.

Salesperson: Do you think that 8 gigabytes is enough to run the software you will be using?

Customer: Yes.

Salesperson: Are you comfortable with the monthly investment schedule?

Customer: Yes.

Salesperson: Then it seems we're all set to go ahead with this installation?

Customer: Yes.

Although the "yes-set" close is fairly easy to understand, many salespeople often fail to apply this effective close. The reason is simple. They are afraid that the buyer will say "no" to any one of the three or four questions they have prepared in advance.

They ask, "How do I deal with a 'no' response to my predictable 'yes' questions?"

No problem: Deal with the "no" response as if you were handling any other objection. Don't act surprised if the prospect says, "No, I don't like the financing terms." Simply inquire, "What terms did you have in mind?"

Handle the objection and continue your "yes-set" close from the top. If your "yes-set" series has been interrupted by an objection, then you need to try a new series of questions. It is for that reason that master sales closers prepare at least six questions that can easily be answered by the prospect with "yes." Some salespeople even prepare a secret checklist as they move through their presentation. For example, they write key words on their notepad like *color, delivery, service, warranty, comfort,* or *financing.*

This little-known preparation step will make the "yes-set" close very easy and safe for you to apply.

On your next sales call, make a deliberate effort to receive as many "yes" responses as you can. Test your ability to stimulate your prospect's mind in a positive way. Discover the amazing power of the "yes-set," and more closes will come automatically.

On the following pages you will find several realistic examples of the "yes-set" close. Customize them for your particular business situation in the space provided.

Tested and Proven "Yes-Set" Closes

1. Is this the kind of quality finish that you had in mind?

[Yes.]

Are you satisfied with the performance data?

[Yes.]

Does the service contract meet your needs?

[Yes.]

Would you like us to deliver this by the end of the month?

[Yes.]

2. Do you like this color more than the others?

[Yes.]

Are you comfortable with the extended warranty that protects your investment for the next five years?

[Yes.]

Would you be able to afford 500 as an initial investment?

[Yes.]

Could you get your checkbook while I prepare the paperwork?

[Yes.]

3. Are you happy with the size of the warehouse?

[Yes.]

Do you like the extra skylights for your office?

[Yes.]

Is this enough square footage for your expansion plans?

[Yes.]

Would you like us to start your building by the 15th so you can move in four months from today?

[Yes.]

4. I bet you were surprised by what this little machine could do.

[Yes.]

Were you satisfied with the lifting capacity?

[Yes.]

Do you feel that this model will help you handle more business so that you will be able to increase your sales volume?

[Yes.]

Can you get the financing?

[Yes.]

Then it sounds like you want us to put one into production for you. Is that right?

[Yes.]

5. Isn't this the kind of car that you always wanted?

[Yes.]

Don't you agree that it is more fun paying for something that you really like than to write a check for something that you hate to drive to work day after day?

[Yes.]

Do you think that a person with your kind of progressive earning power can afford a commitment of $800 a month?

[Yes.]

May I say congratulations, because you're getting an exceptionally beautiful new car that you'll be proud to own?

[Yes.]

6. Didn't you tell me earlier that operating speed was one of your prime concerns prior to this demonstration?

[Yes.]

Were you satisfied with the way this mailing machine handled the 200 letters in less than two minutes?

[Yes.]

Do you agree with my figures that this feature alone is bound to save you about one hour per day?

[Yes.]

Well, if we figure 200 working days in a year and one hour at $10, this savings alone would amount to about $2,000. Am I correct?

[Yes.]

And in five years, we're talking about a savings of $10,000. Right?

[Yes.]

Since the total investment in this machine is only $5,000, it would be reasonable to say that this machine not only pays for itself, but it will actually make a profit of $5,000, right?

[Yes.]

I believe that this is the kind of investment that you have been looking for. Right?

[Yes.]

Shall we go ahead with the paperwork now?
[Yes.]

7. Is it important to you to increase your visibility in this particular market?
[Yes.]

Are you able to follow up on the new leads this advertising program is bound to generate for you?
[Yes.]

Do you like the copy approach of this ad?
[Yes.]

Are we in agreement that a spot color would make your ad stand out from the crowd?
[Yes.]

Do I have your okay to confirm this schedule with our head office today?
[Yes.]

8. Are 48 extensions enough for this telephone system?
[Yes.]

Do you like the conference call features?

[Yes.]

Is it important to you to have a backup system in case there is a power failure?

[Yes.]

Then it sounds like the M54 series is the one that suits your needs best. Am I correct?

[Yes.]

Would you like us to install this for you by the end of the month?

[Yes.]

9. _____

_____

_____

10. _____

_____

_____

CHAPTER 4

The Objection Close

Objections are questions in disguise.

- "Your Price Is Too High!"
- "I Have to Think About It!"
- How an IBM Salesman Turned Indifference into a Close
- Thirteen Objections You Can't Overcome During a Sale

Customer Objections Are Buying Signals

A master sales closer in the construction equipment industry, who is also an enthusiastic mountain climber, once told me: "A prospect who objects is like an impressive rock ledge with wide cracks and solid footholds. There is plenty of room in which to wedge your shoes and get a firm grip. The prospect who doesn't tell you where you stand is the one you have to worry about because he's letting you slide as if you were trying to climb a mountain of whipped cream."

Objections Are Ideal Opportunities for Closing

As a general rule, the prospect who objects is the one who buys. However, there is one condition: that you first handle the objection.

The three toughest customer objections are:

1. Indifference (no need)

2. Price (no money)

3. Procrastination (no hurry)

> **Objections are nothing but questions in disguise . . . and ideal opportunities to close.**

All three are ideal opportunities for closing the sale. The key for handling each one of these objections lies in interpreting the prospect's objection as a request for additional information.

- Translate "no need" into: "Prove that I will benefit from your product or service."
- Translate "no money" into: "Show me how this product will pay for itself."
- Translate "no hurry" into: "Explain how I can win by buying now."

This Special Card Game Can Boost Your Objection-Handling Skills

Handling objections requires skills, courage, and sometimes even audacity. Salespeople often complain about their inability to think of a quick answer when they hear an objection in the customer's office. However, right after they leave, they always think of several good comebacks that could have closed the deal.

To improve your ability to handle objections quickly and effectively, here is a powerful practice drill:

Write 12 typical customer objections on 3- by 5-inch cards. Shuffle the cards and turn them face down on the table before you. Next, begin your memorized sales presentation. Go through it as if you were actually talking to your prospect.

After a few minutes, turn over the first card and interrupt yourself with the objection written on the card. Read it out loud and handle the objection on the spot. Then get back on track with your sales presentation.

After a few minutes, interrupt yourself again and repeat the process until you've covered every one of your objection cards.

This skills-building card game will help you think on your feet, and it will also help you learn how to keep control of the interview no matter what the interruption.

Update your objection cards and repeat this game often. It will help you close more sales.

"Your Price Is Too High!"

1. I agree, our price is higher because this is a higher-quality product. That brings up a question: Are you very rich? [Wait for inevitable "no" reply.]

The reason I am asking is because only the very rich can afford to buy a low-quality product. They have the money to buy a new one every time it breaks. You see, I'd like to help you save money by buying this one. You'll save money because it will last.

2. I understand how you feel. It appears a little high, yet we sell over 2,800 units per year at these very same prices. Doesn't that tell you something? You know better than I that if our customers did not think that this was a profitable investment, we would never be able to sell that many.

3. I am surprised to hear that you feel that way. How do you compare the price? [Wait for answer, then explain how your product offers a higher value.]

4. That is exactly the reason why you should buy today. We are expecting another price increase any day. I'd like to help you save money by ordering now.

5. What price are you referring to, the original investment or the cost per hour of use? [Wait for reply.] I can appreciate your saying that. However, when you look at the longer life of our product, your cost per hour of use will be significantly lower.

6. Let me ask you a question. Do you like your watch? [Wait for predictable "yes" reply.] I thought you would say that because it is a very elegant timepiece. Did you buy it for yourself? [Wait for "yes" reply, then continue.] Do you happen to remember exactly how much you paid for this watch, including the sales tax? [Chances are that your prospect won't remember the exact price.] You see, here is my point: You are enjoying this watch for a much longer time than you can remember its price. I believe that today you don't regret having made this investment, correct? [Wait for positive response.] And I would guess that today, you don't miss the money you've spent either. Right? [Wait for affirmative reply.] Well, I believe that we are in a similar situation now. You won't miss the money you'll invest in this product just as you don't miss the money you've paid to get your watch!

7. Is that the only reason that prevents you from buying now? [If client says "no," ask for additional reason behind objection. If prospect says "yes," put a specific dollar value on every single customer benefit to justify the price.]

8. You know the old saying: Good things aren't cheap, and cheap things aren't good.

9. Yes, the price seems high, but only when you think of what you have to pay. It seems low when you think of what you will get.

10. This product may cost a little more than others; however, you get a lot more quality. As a result, it will last longer and maintain its value longer.

11. _____

_____

_____

12. _____

_____

_____

_____

"I Have to Think About It!"

1. I can see that this is a difficult decision for you. What is it that you want to think about?

2. I understand that you need more time. Before you decide one way or another, would you tell me the reasons for and the reasons against going ahead with this proposal?

3. Is it the product or the price you need to think about? [Isolate the objection.]

4. Obviously you must have a reason for saying that. Would you mind telling me what it is?

5. Is there something about me that prevents you from thinking about this now?

6. Let me ask you a question: What will it take to do business with you today?

7. That's no problem. I can help you with that. I don't want you to buy this until you're 100 percent convinced that this is indeed the best choice for you. Where do you feel we are now? At about 80 percent? [Wait for "yes."] What do we need to do to earn the additional 20 percent? What kind of evidence would you need to feel 100 percent secure?

8. Great. I encourage that. Let's review what you like about this proposal while it is fresh in your mind . . .

9. Of course you do. Many of my customers have spent as much as a year thinking about buying. You know that every one of them

CHAPTER 4

keeps telling me that they wished they had bought sooner.

10. _____

_____

_____

11. _____

_____

_____

How an IBM Salesman Turned Indifference into a Close

Robert Z. Wilkinson was working as a marketing representative for IBM in Portland, Oregon, when he made a sales call to a difficult customer. As he entered the front door, he requested a brief interview with Mr. Smith (not his real name).

Robert smiled and handed a business card to the receptionist. She told him in a chilly tone of voice that she would inform Mr. Smith that he wished to see him. She disappeared into Mr. Smith's office and closed the door. A moment later the door opened and the receptionist returned. She handed back the card that had been torn in half and said sadly, "Mr. Smith didn't say anything, but I don't think he wants to see you today."

Undaunted, Robert asked her if he could borrow her stapler. As she watched, he stapled his card back together with a neat row of three staples down the middle. Then he ran a row of staples around the outside edges of the card so that each staple just overlapped the previous one. With this kind of reinforcement, it would be hard for anyone to tear that card again.

The marketing rep asked the receptionist if she would mind going back to Mr. Smith to apologize for having such a flimsy business card and to request a 10-minute appointment. She took the stapled card, went back to Mr. Smith's office, and closed the door. After a few tense moments, Robert noticed Mr. Smith peeking around the door, holding his stapled card, and chuckling, "You, from IBM, come on in, you've earned your 10 minutes."

Needless to say, Robert made a new friend and got the sale.

Thirteen Objections You Can't Overcome During a Sale

Below are 13 poor sales habits that can cause you to lose the opportunity for closing the sale:

> **The toughest objection is the one you don't recognize because you've created it.**

1. Poor appearance

2. Long-winded presentations (talking too much and sidetracking)

3. Nervousness, insecurity, hesitancy

4. Lack of planning every step of the sale

5. Lack of clarity and focus

6. Lack of enthusiasm and courage

CHAPTER 4

7. Failure to identify customer's needs

8. Too eager to close (high-pressure selling)

9. Criticizing competition or the customer's ideas

10. Ignoring objections or giving weak answers

11. Failure to establish value

12. Courting prospects who are afraid to say "no," and failing to pin them down

13. Failure to ask for the order

CHAPTER 5

The Persuasion Close

Sell the sizzle, not the steak.

- Help Your Prospects Imagine How Their Dreams Will Come True
- Illustrate How Nightmares Can Turn into Reality
- Explain to Your Prospects What They Will Save by Deciding Now

What Do Your Customers Really Buy?

Although countless books have been written about the power of persuasion in selling, many salespeople are confused about why their customers really buy their product.

To find a new answer to this key question, I talked to several authorities in the field.

A very well known sales seminar leader told me that he too had pondered the questions and wondered why about 80 percent of the people who bought his CDs during the seminar would never listen to them even once.

> **The most powerful movers of people are dreams.**

A master sales closer in the powerboat business shared the same bewilderment. He observed that many customers invested thousands of dollars in luxurious cruising boats, yet on a beautiful weekend he never saw more than 20 percent of the boats leave the marina.

An accomplished speaker and bestselling coauthor spent part of his selling career in the business of selling vegetable slicers. When he demonstrated his handy kitchen device, people would instantly recognize the benefits and promptly sign the order. When he delivered the slicer, he again demonstrated its use and would leave the machines on the countertop. Over time, he realized that the next day, most people would store the tool under the counter and leave it there unused for years to come.

Why did these people buy products that they didn't use? The answer is that people don't buy products—they buy dream fulfillment.

A smart Rolls-Royce sales rep in Palm Beach, Florida, considered herself to be in the business of selling dreams. "I know it is foolish to spend $165,000 on a car that the owner will drive no more than 3,000 miles a year. But if that's what it takes to give the owner pleasure and meaning, then that's what I ought to be selling," she said.

Your prospect's dreams should be part of your closing strategy. No matter how foolish that dream may seem to you, it is precious to the prospect—therefore, it is vital to your close.

> **The biggest closing secret is to ask for the order early and often.**

People Are Influenced by Words That Evoke Dreams

Master sales closers know that the most powerful movers of people are dreams. A single dream can ruin a good night's sleep, or change your life. If you listen to what people dream about, you can begin to influence them. If your sales presentation is built around the promise that you will make your prospect's dreams come true, you will close the sale. The makers of dreams believe in their own magic, and your promises.

The sales seminar leader who sells motivational CDs evokes the dream of reaching success; the powerboat sales rep sells the dream of relaxation and fun; the kitchen appliance salesperson sells the dream of healthier meals.

CHAPTER 5

The biggest secret to persuasive selling lies in reading other people's dreams and helping them fulfill these dreams. In other words, if you want your dreams to come true, you need to help other people make their dreams come true.

Here Are Three Successful Persuasion Strategies for Closing More Sales Today

1.   Help your prospects imagine how their dreams will come true when they buy.

2.   Illustrate how nightmares can turn into reality if your prospects do not buy your product or service.

3.   Explain to your prospects what they will save by making the decision now.

On the following pages you will find easy-to-use examples of these powerful closing techniques.

Help Your Prospects Imagine How Their Dreams Will Come True

1.   *Selling a telephone system.* Imagine for a moment that you make this investment today. In less than one week you will be able to use your speakerphone, you will save time with this automatic redial button, and your staff will enjoy the intercom features and congratulate you on making this great decision. Isn't that a solution that will make everybody happy?

2.   *Selling industrial products.* Let's say that you agree to this deal; here is what I see a month from now. You are walking out to your warehouse, and you see your forklift operator stacking the pallets up to the highest level of your warehouse. Your plant manager walks over with a big smile on his face. He tells you that in the last 30 days productivity has increased by 35 percent. He knows that this was possible only because of that great investment you've made. Isn't that what you'd like to see happen?

3. *Selling pharmaceutical products.* I can see you prescribing this new antibiotic to about 10 patients during the course of next week. A week later you will hear the happy comments from your patients. The reason I am saying this is because this new drug acts twice as fast as conventional prescriptions, and there are fewer side-effects. I know that you will be pleased you made the decision to give this new product a try.

> **Turn prospects into dreamers... it helps you close sales.**

4. _____

_____

_____

5. _____

_____

_____

Illustrate How Nightmares Can Turn into Reality

1. *Industrial sales.* You told me earlier that your business is expanding and that you need to increase your production capacity. If you leave things the way they are, you may no longer be competitive, and you may lose more business than what it would cost to make this investment now. I don't think you want to run that risk. Am I correct?

2. *Financial sales.* Mr. Brown, one of my clients, was in a similar situation a few months ago. He decided that it would be best for him to wait a few weeks until the interest rates came down a little more. You know what happened? [Pause.] The prime rate went up by a point, and at the same time we had a 3 percent price increase. I don't mean to sound negative, and I don't want to say you can't afford to wait, but buying now means that you'll avoid these unnecessary losses.

3. *Office equipment sales.* Suppose your copier breaks down just when you want to get an important report copied for your board of directors meeting. Can you imagine what your boss will say to you? [Pause.] I think that you want things to get better, not worse . . . right?

> **Never underestimate the motivating power of fear.**

4. _____

_____

_____

5. _____

_____

_____

Explain to Your Prospects What They Will Save by Deciding Now

1. If you order now, you will save $450. This model is on sale only until Friday, and we can't guarantee that our inventory will last. Would you like to save $450 today?

2. You will be pleased to know that you can still get this product at the old price. Our new price list will come in on Monday, so you are saving 5 percent if you get it today.

3. If you order this now, I can give you the larger model for the same price. It is a terrific product and a great buy. Don't you agree?

4. Starting next week, we will have to add delivery charges. Don't you think it would be better to get your order in today so that you won't have to pay extra?

5. Have you read the article in our industry publication about the shortages of this item? If I were in your shoes, I'd plan for a larger order so that you don't run the risk of having to cut your production. We can still guarantee you a six-month supply if we call in your order today.

6. This car is our bestselling model. There are only two in our inventory. Any new models will have a $250 surcharge on top of the sticker price. If I were you, I would write a deposit check to put one on hold. Let me help you save $250, and let's get the ball rolling.

7. Mrs. Smith, your car will never be worth more than it is today. Right now your trade-in value is $6,400. When you come back next month, you may have a transmission problem, a small dent in the door, and another 2,000 miles on the odometer. That's not going to increase your trade-in value. You know the old saying: "Buy low, sell high." You bought your car at a low price, and we're paying you the highest possible trade-in dollar. Isn't this a good enough reason to trade now?

8. You have studied our proposal very carefully. We have agreed that it meets your needs. We have only one unit left in our inventory. If it goes to another customer, we can't guarantee the same price. Why don't you protect yourself against paying more and take this last one. I know that next week you will be glad you made the decision to buy today. Shall I call our warehouse today?

9. _____

_____

_____

10. _____

_____

_____

CHAPTER 6

The Summary Close

Help your prospect refocus and buy.

- How to Introduce Your Summary Close with a Smooth Transition Statement
- How to Reconfirm Your Prospect's Specific Needs
- How to Summarize Your Features and Benefits to Match Your Prospect's Needs
- How to Ask For the Order in No Uncertain Terms
- Eight Ways to Win with the Summary Close
- How to Add Extra Impact to Your Summary Close
- The T-Account Summary Close

How the Summary Close Works

When you approach the end of your sales presentation, your prospect is faced with the task of organizing all the individual pieces of information you've given him or her into one clear and comprehensive picture.

Although your prospects may be impressed with your vast amount of knowledge, they may experience some difficulty with organizing what you have told them.

In essence, the summary close is designed to refocus your prospects' thinking on a composite picture of those parts of your presentation that clearly fit their needs.

Amateur salespeople tend to think of the summary close as a quick review of what they like about the product. They fail to match the summary close to the buyer's specific situation and then wonder why the prospect didn't buy.

There are four separate steps to a successful summary close:

1. Introduce your summary close with a smooth transition statement.

2. Briefly reconfirm your prospect's specific needs.

3. Summarize how your features and benefits meet your prospect's needs.

4. Ask for the order in no uncertain terms.

On the following pages you will find specific illustrations of all four steps to develop successful summary closes.

How to Introduce Your Summary Close with a Smooth Transition Statement

Here are some tested selling sentences that have been used by master sales closers to create an elegant transition from the sales presentation to the summary close:

1. At this point, I'd like to review what we've discussed so that we can find out if there are still open questions in your mind.

2. Why don't we take a moment to review some of the key points and see how they fit your particular situation. Would that be okay with you?

3. I think we've covered a lot of information in a fairly short time. Would you agree to spend a couple of minutes to review the essential points?

_4._ May I suggest that we take a step back and look at the big picture?

_5._ Before you make up your mind one way or another, let's take a moment to review the key points of our solution.

_6._ Before we get lost in too many details, why don't we take a minute now and summarize what we've discussed so far.

_7._ We've covered a lot of areas today. Would it be all right with you to review the highlights of this proposal?

8. _____

_____

_____

9. _____

_____

_____

How to Reconfirm Your Prospect's Specific Needs

When you rephrase your prospect's needs, you demonstrate your most important professional attribute—you show that you've listened.

1. You mentioned earlier that you wanted a machine that was faster, cheaper, and easier to operate. Have I got that right?

2. If I remember correctly, you are interested in a plan that will give you higher coverage, fewer administrative problems, and lower monthly payments. Was there anything else?

3. I believe you told me that there were four essential factors that you would be looking at: more comfort, lower maintenance cost, higher productivity, and better service support. Is that correct?

4. When we discussed your specifications for your new addition, you outlined several critical points that were important to you. One was an improved overall design. Then you mentioned easier access and a better traffic flow. Of course, the overall cost was supposed to fit your reduced budget for this fiscal year. Am I right?

5. You want a car that is fast, safe, and easy to maintain. And of course, you want it at the lowest price. Do we agree?

6. You've told me that you need 2 gigabytes of hard drive space, 40 megabytes of RAM, and a high-speed modem. Have I left anything out?

7. _____

_____

_____

8. _____

_____

_____

How to Summarize Your Features and Benefits to Match Your Prospect's Needs

1. There are four essential reasons why our model 120 is clearly the best choice for your special situation. First, you get 30 percent more power; second, the operating comfort is obviously much greater; third, you will have a 15 percent savings in maintenance cost; and the fourth and most important benefit to you is that you will be able to increase your overall productivity by at least 25 percent.

2. You remember discussing the fact that this new plan will give you higher coverage in all essential areas. We also confirmed that the administrative procedures have been streamlined to a point where you practically eliminate 50 percent of your paperwork. But the best feature is that this proposal will cut your monthly payments by $235.

3. You have seen how we've increased the horsepower over last year's model. I believe you used the word *dynamite* when I told you about it. You also noticed our new maintenance guidelines, and you have seen how much time you will be saving in this area. Then we talked about the 24-hour service hotline where you get all the assistance you need to avoid unnecessary downtime. This way you can easily stay ahead of your production goals.

4. _____

_____

_____

5. _____

_____

_____

How to Ask For the Order in No Uncertain Terms

After summarizing your key benefits, it is most likely that your prospect's interest has reached a peak interest level. At this point it is vital not to sidetrack or to raise additional points of discussion. You've arrived at the most critical phase, so go ahead and pop the question!

1. When would you like us to start putting this plan into motion?

2. Isn't this the kind of savings that you want in your business? [Wait for "yes."] I figured that you would say that. Would you please initial our agreement?

3. Considering these savings, the only question you need to answer is: When you would like us to install it?

4. Since we've agreed that this product will meet your needs perfectly and since you have seen how this product practically pays for itself, shall we go ahead and schedule production for May delivery?

5. I am glad we had a chance to review how well our new plan fits your particular situation. Would you please confirm this deal?

6. Isn't this a perfect fit? What amount shall we figure as the down payment?

7. These are the three most important reasons for you to go ahead with this purchase. Can we put them down on paper?

8. _____

_____

_____

9. _____

_____

_____

Eight Ways to Win with the Summary Close

1. Instead of repeating what you've said before, condense your best points in a compelling way.

2. Don't summarize with statements alone—always ask questions that involve your prospect.

3. If you are selling face-to-face, don't limit your summary to verbal expressions; use visuals to illustrate your words. (See page 89.)

4.   Always repeat your prospect's positive words; they will increase your prospect's motivation to buy.

5.   Choose your benefit statements carefully. Select benefits that add value, choose benefits that eliminate fear, and use benefits that add excitement.

6.   Always remember that the most important part of the word *benefit* consists of the last three letters: *f-i-t*. These three letters mean that your product must "fit" your customer's needs. Without these three letters, your benefits will be meaningless to your prospect.

7. Repeat your prospect's positive statements about your product to rekindle your own excitement about closing the sale.

8. Always bring the summary close to a comfortable and satisfying conclusion with a direct question.

How to Add Extra Impact to Your Summary Close

During face-to-face sales calls, you can increase your chances for a sale by writing your key benefits on a notepad. This close works best when you encourage your customer to participate in developing the summary.

"Mr. Smith, I'd like to get your objective opinion on some of the items we've discussed so far. What do you think of the operator comfort? Do you think it will increase productivity?"

When the prospect answers "yes," you write on a pad: Increased productivity.

"How about the lower cost per hour. Is that important to you?"

If the prospect say "yes," write: Lower cost per hour.

"How do you feel about the extended warranty? Would you consider this as an important safety factor that will protect your investment?"

If you hear a "yes," you add the following words to your list: Safe investment.

If you hear a "no," move on to the next item.

"I believe we've agreed earlier that the higher operating speed will increase your production capacity by 25 percent. Am I correct?"

After you hear your prospect's "yes," add the following words: 25 percent increased production.

After you have obtained four or five confirmations to your customer benefits, you summarize with these words:

"Mr. Smith, it appears that what you will get is increased productivity [put checkmark next to first item], lower cost per hour, a safe investment, and a 25 percent increase in production. Would you like me to check with the factory when we could deliver one to you?"

The T-Account Summary Close

This close is also known as the "Ben Franklin" close. You simply draw a large T across the page while telling your prospect:

"Mr. Smith, in order to weigh the benefits against the possible disadvantages of owning this product, let's take a moment and see what they are." [Start by writing a big plus sign on the upper left corner and a minus sign on the right side.]

"We've mentioned the increased productivity; then we have agreed how much faster our product operates. That represents a 23 percent gain in speed. Correct? We've also agreed that maintenance will be easier and that you'll get six hours of free training."

Pause, look at the prospect, and ask, "What would you say are the reasons that speak against buying this now?" [Hand your summary to the prospect.] In many situations, the prospect will say "None," and you've just concluded the sale!

+	−
23% faster	
Easier maintenance	
Free training	

CHAPTER 7

The Alternative Close

Make buying a natural selection process.

- Choices between Products
- Choices between Modes of Payment
- Choices between Different Modes of Delivery
- Choices between Different Types of Installation
- Choices between Different Incentives

How the Alternative Close Works

In essence, the alternative close successfully concludes the sale by asking the prospect to choose between two or more alternatives.

The beautiful part of this technique is that no matter which alternative your customer chooses, the sale is yours.

This closing technique offers a 50 percent higher chance for success than the single-question close, providing that your customer has been appropriately primed for the alternative close.

The basic technique involved in this close is very simple, which leads many salespeople to brush aside the need for preparing for this effective closing approach. Just as a builder begins a building by creating a solid foundation, master sales closers begin their alternative close by constructing a similar structure.

How to Build the Foundation for the

Alternative Close

The alternative close works best by presenting your prospect with a smorgasbord of minor choices throughout the sales process. This method will get your prospect accustomed to picking alternatives, and by the time you ask the final question, you can be certain to get a satisfactory answer.

To get your prospect into the habit of choosing between two or more alternatives, you must prepare a series of alternative questions. Each time your prospect responds to one of your choices, show how pleased you are with his or her response.

Example:

Salesperson: Are you planning to use this product in your office or at home?

Customer: In my office.

Salesperson: Great! [Smile.] Would you be the one to operate this product, or would you be sharing this with others?

Customer: I would share this with two other people.

Salesperson: That's a smart plan. [Smile.] Do you think that there will be more users during the next three years, or do you think that the number will stay about the same?

Customer: I think we'll add two more people next year.

Salesperson: Oh, you seem to be growing rapidly. [Pleased.] Shall we go over some of the basic choices that are available to you that I think will fit your needs?

Customer: Go right ahead.

This example illustrates how a master closer presents a series of alternatives throughout the presentation. The prospect gets into the habit of selecting the one he or she likes best. In response, the salesperson offers positive feedback to reward the customer for making a choice. You can do that with a slight head nod, a smile, or a friendly comment. This way you will build the necessary psychological momentum, to ensure you get a positive response to your final, alternative closing question. Master sales closers know that without this preparatory work, the alternative close is bound to encounter unexpected resistance.

Summary of Steps to Prepare Your Customer for the Alternative Close

1. Get your prospect in the habit of choosing between alternatives throughout your presentation.

2. Reward your customer with positive feedback after each response.

3. Ask the final, alternative closing question.

Choices between Products

1. Would you prefer to keep this demonstrator model at the reduced price, or would you like to get a brand-new one?

2. You have three options to choose from, the red finish, the gold-plated, and the silver. Which one do you think will fit best for your office?

3. The 190 model has 150 horsepower, the 220 has 30 percent more. Would you like the one that has more muscle?

4. Would 16 lines fit your expansion plans, or would you prefer to go with 24?

5. Do you really think the standard version will fit your style, or would you prefer the more advanced deluxe product?

6. _____

_____

_____

7. _____

_____

_____

Choices between Modes of Payment

1. Do you feel comfortable with the lease plan, or do you prefer to finance this with your bank?

2. We would be happy to defer billing until the end of the month and give you 30-day terms, or you can pay cash and get this software program free. What choice would you prefer?

3. Would you like to charge this to Visa or MasterCard?

4. I'll be happy to take your check now, or would you prefer us to send it COD?

5. Can we send you a bill, or would you prefer us to add the amount to your next statement?

6. _____
_____
_____

7. _____
_____
_____

Choices between Different Modes of Delivery

1. For a small charge, we could have this delivered overnight, but if you'd like to save a few dollars, we can have it shipped as slower freight, and you'll have it in one week. Which way would fit your plans best?

2. You have two options concerning delivery. One would be by rail—that's the more economical, but it will take three weeks. Or it can be shipped by truck, and that's the faster way, but it will be $150 extra in freight. How soon would you need it?

3. We could send this by Federal Express, or would you like to save a few dollars and wait for the mail?

4. If you are in a rush, we could send our courier this afternoon, or would you prefer to pick it up yourself?

5. _____
_____
_____

6. _____
_____
_____

Choices between Different Types of Installation

1. When you install this unit, you will need a skilled mechanic to connect the couplings. Do you prefer to do this job with your people, or shall we plan to send out our site engineer with the delivery truck?

2. Our service includes free installation. However, this special model requires a temperature-controlled room. Would you like us to install the climate control too, or would you prefer to have your building engineer take care of this?

3. Do you want us to install your expansion board, or would you like to save and do it yourself?

4. Would you like us to add the security
system when we install your stereo, or
would you prefer to go ahead without it?

5. _____
_____
_____

6. _____
_____
_____

Choices between Different Incentives

1. There are two ways to save money. You can take your usual order of a dozen at the discounted price, or you can take two dozen and get this beautiful display free. What would be your preference today?

2. These monitors are $300 each. If you order 5, you can get 1 free. Would you like to take this special offer, or would you be satisfied with only 5—or would 10 be better?

3. If you take a dozen, you get 1 free; if you take 20, you get 2 free. What would you prefer?

4. Each individual item is $50; if you get all three, you'll get a 10 percent discount. Would you like a set of three?

5. _____

_____

_____

6. _____

_____

_____

CHAPTER 8

The Price Close

Build value before quoting the price.

- Begin Your Price Close by Begging the Question
- Always Add a Little Suspense before Quoting Your Price
- Always Present Your Price with Pride . . . It Pays!
- How to Justify Your Price and Your Profit Margin
- The Four Basic Ways to Present Your Price
- When You Present Your Price, Never Follow the Rules. Make Your Own Rules!
- Make Your Price Comparisons More Memorable
- Advertising Is Cheaper by the Dozen
- How to Close the Sale by Negotiating Small Price Concessions

Begin Your Price Close by Begging the Question

Prospects often pressure salespeople to discuss the price of the product or service long before they can begin to fathom the value they will receive in return for their money.

Master sales closers are skilled in deferring price questions so that they can continue to build value in their prospect's mind before quoting the price.

Here are some tested techniques for postponing price questions:

1. Mr. Smith, I am glad you asked me that question. I will come to it in a minute.

2. Mrs. Brown, it really depends on how you are going to purchase it. I'll figure that for you in a few moments.

3. Tom, let's discuss if you can use it first, before we figure out what it will cost.

4. Kathy, I appreciate your interest in the financial side of this proposal. May I get back to that in a couple of minutes?

5. Could we put this question on hold for now? I'll be glad to put all the figures together for you in a moment.

6. At this point I could give you only a ballpark figure, but once we have established what you really need, I'll be happy to give you a detailed quote.

7. Mr. Simon, our price is the best part of our product. Let me save this for last, okay? [Smile.]

8. _____

_____

_____

9. _____

_____

_____

Always Add a Little Suspense before Quoting Your Price

The timing of your price quote is just as important as the timing of your close. If you quote your price too soon, you may have to face unnecessary objections. If you hold out for too long, your customer may become annoyed and lose interest.

Here are some polished techniques collected from top closers:

1. Before I explain the price to you, I want you to know that this is the latest model, and it has the most advanced features available today.

2. Before I tell you how much this model sells for, I'd like to point out to you that it contains a brand-new device that will reduce your operating cost by 30 percent.

3. Please remember that this model is much better and more efficient than the old one.

You see, it has three significant improvements. [Explain them one at a time.]

4. I believe that you are aware that this is our hottest product. It is so much in demand just because it is much easier to operate.

5. Everybody is amazed at how this new feature improved the performance of this product.

6. This single improvement alone can pay for this product within the next two years of operation.

7. _____
_____
_____

8. _____
_____
_____

Always Present Your Price with Pride...It Pays!

Your customers tend to respect your positive attitude about price, but they will often try to chisel you if they sense hesitation or lack of confidence.

Many years ago, Ed McMahon, the famous entertainer and TV personality, sold fountain pens on the boardwalk in Atlantic City. Before he quoted his price, he would hold up his pen as if it were a valuable piece of jewelry. His body language communicated value and pride. He became one of the top sales closers in this highly competitive field.

Here are some effective sample scripts for presenting price with pride:

1. I know that the figure I am going to quote you is much higher than what you had in mind. However, keep in mind that this product is going to help you make much more money than you figured.

2. I just want you to know that the price of this product may shock you. But, of course, we are talking about one of the best investments you can make.

3. If you haven't been in the market for a _____ lately, then you may get a little sticker shock. But you also will get a pleasant surprise when you see what this machine will do for you.

4. Our prices are not the cheapest. However, nobody can offer you more for your money than we can.

5. _____

_____

_____

6. _____

_____

_____

How to Justify Your Price and Your Profit Margin

Many customers attempt to negotiate for a price cut on the absurd speculation that your profit margin ought to be slashed to what they feel is a more reasonable level. Your pride in your price demands that you respond firmly and with self-respect by asserting your right to profits.

1. Yes, our price includes a reasonable profit margin. Our profit is your insurance that we will continue to stay in business so we can take care of your service and maintenance problems throughout the lifetime of your product.

2. I believe you agree that there is no sense in taking an order without making a profit. Would you trust a company that makes a habit of losing money?

3. You know better than I do that if a company lowers the price, the cut has to come from somewhere. Would you want us to shave off a little from your warranty? Would you want us to shave off a little from our service when you need it? Or would you want us to shave off a little from our parts inventory? I don't believe you would want us to do any of these things. Am I correct?

4. You see, when you buy this product, we will make a small profit. But we make this profit only once. Your profit will be continuous. You will be able to use this product for several years, and each year it will add to your profits.

5. If we were to cut the price, where should we cut it from? You agree that it has to come from somewhere. [Wait for reply.] Well, it can't come from our profit because we need it to stay in business. It can't come from our expenses because they are fixed. It can't come from our costs because they are set by our suppliers. You see, there is no way we can make any cuts.

6. Our modest profit is far less than the added value we offer. We offer you a quality product, dependable service, and a high reputation for on-time delivery, and we have earned the respect of our customers for standing behind our workmanship 100 percent.

7. When you compare all the different models and prices, you will need to realize that our profit pays for the high-quality service staff you will be dealing with. There are few companies that will agree to sell at a loss. However, when it comes to service, you may be at a loss too.

8. _____
_____
_____

9. _____
_____
_____

The Four Basic Ways to Present Your Price

1. *Present your price by adding up your benefits.* Mr. Smith, our price includes the following items: the basic unit, plus the automatic control panel, plus a one-year service contract, plus installation and delivery. You will get the most dependable model, the most advanced features, and the most productive system for only $7,500.

2. *Subtract the savings from your total price.* Over a five-year period you can deduct $2,000 in lower fuel consumption. You also save about $1,000 on spare parts because of the new design. When you figure these savings in relation to your investment of $29,000, your total extra benefit package amounts to a 10 percent discount.

3. *Present your price by multiplying your benefits.* This unit will save you $5 per hour on electricity. Since you will be operating this unit for 60 hours a week, you will save $300 per week. If we figure 50 weeks of production, your savings in electricity alone will be $15,000 a year. Now isn't that alone a good enough reason to go ahead with this investment?

4. *Present your price by dividing it into small units.* Since the average life expectancy for this equipment is five years, your total investment of $1,500 translates to about $1 a day. That's so little that you'll never miss it.

5. _____

_____

_____

6. _____

_____

_____

_____

When You Present Your Price, Never Follow the Rules. Make Your Own Rules!

Every industry has its particular way of presenting the final cost of a product or service. In the printing industry, most salespeople follow the rule of quoting each job on a cost-per-thousand basis. For example, the cost for 25,000 envelopes would be quoted at $1,125. Then the salesperson would divide that cost and say, "Your cost per 1,000 is only $45."

The problem with following the practiced standard is that your offer won't stand out in your customer's mind, and the buying decision will always be made on the lowest cost-per-thousand figure.

Make Your Price Comparisons More Memorable

A master sales closer in the printing industry developed the creative technique of dividing the cost into a smaller number and then comparing this small number to something his prospects would understand better.

For example, a quote for 25,000 envelopes is presented like this:

"Mr. Smith, we would be pleased to print the 25,000 envelopes you need for exactly four and a half cents apiece. In other words, we'll produce and deliver high-quality envelopes to you for about half the price."

Advertising Is Cheaper by the Dozen

In the advertising business, many salespeople follow the standard rule of translating the advertising cost per page into the cost per 1,000 readers.

For example, a sales rep of a magazine with a circulation of 100,000 and a single-page rate of $4,000 would translate the advertising budget into a cost of $40 per 1,000 readers.

A top sales closer in the advertising field has successfully tested a new method of presenting the cost of one page of advertising with these words:

"With our publication your ad will reach 100,000 subscribers. The investment for a one-page ad is $4,000, which as you know amounts to only 48 cents for a dozen readers. You see, it is really very inexpensive to deliver your message to 12 qualified prospects for less than what it costs to mail two letters."

How to Close the Sale by Negotiating Small Price Concessions

Master sales closers follow the tested negotiation rule "Never make the first offer." They let their customers tell them before-hand what figure they had in mind. Next, they may offer a very small concession, but with one hitch—that the customer first agrees to the deal.

1. May I use your phone to check if there is any chance of getting you that special deal? [Wait for "yes" answer, dial a few digits of your office number, then stop.] But wait a minute, what if he says "no"? If I can persuade him to split the difference, will you agree?

2. If I can get my head office to accept your request for free delivery, do we have a deal?

3. If our production department approves delivery without this feature, so we can reduce your investment commitment, will you okay this purchase today?

4. If I could get a higher allowance for your trade-in from my manager, would you be willing to write a deposit check now?

5. We have never written an order for such a low figure. If I can get my sales manager to go along with this deal, would you be prepared to sign the papers today?

6. I am sorry, but we can't change the price. However, we might be able to get you a better interest rate. What would you say if I asked my financing department to consider prime plus 2?

7. I believe that there is a way we can meet your needs. If I am not mistaken, we have one model in the warehouse that has been scratched. It's brand new. We may be able to sell you this at about $300 off list. Would you want this one, provided it is still there?

8. There is nothing that I can do about the price. However, we might consider helping you with the payment terms. If I can get this approved, will you make this investment?

9. I know from our plant manager that we had a repossession due to a bankruptcy. The product is brand new, with only four operating hours. Let's suppose that I can let you have that one at a special price. Would you take it?

10. There is absolutely nothing that I can do about the price. The only thing we would consider is deferred billing. Would you want me to check this out for you?

11. I just spoke to my sales manager, and we would consider absorbing the freight charges if you would be willing to increase your initial deposit by 15 percent. Do we have a deal?

12. _____
_____
_____

13. _____
_____
_____

CHAPTER 9

The Analogy Close

Add clarity and focus to your close.

- How Interactive Analogies Help You Close More Sales
- How the Speeding-Car Analogy Can Get Your Buyer to Act
- How the *Titanic* Analogy Can Sell Superior Quality
- How the Employment Analogy Can Overcome Price Resistance
- How the Sailboat Analogy Can Save Your Sale from the Budget Ax
- How the Iceberg Analogy Can Sell Your Superior Service
- Your Own Analogy Close

Why Use an Analogy?

The purpose of using an analogy is to clarify an unfamiliar point with a familiar illustration. The analogy will help your prospect to make new mental connections that lead to greater understanding. The right analogy will often get your prospect to share your point of view and then purchase the product.

There are two types of analogies that can drive your selling points home and close the sale:

1. Common analogies

2. Interactive analogies

Average sales producers use common analogies such as these:

"This is the Cadillac of the industry."

"This warranty is as good as gold."

"This product is built like a Sherman tank."

"This machine is as fast as lightning."

Although common analogies can add interest to your closing process, they need additional closing action (such as trial closes) in order to conclude the deal.

For example, a salesperson might say: "This is the Cadillac of the industry. I assume that you are interested in owning a product that offers superior quality. Am I correct?"

This common analogy is bound to work well in most selling situations, yet this approach is all too often overused. If your customers are becoming resistant to these common analogies, then you may want to use the following more advanced techniques.

How Interactive Analogies Help You Close More Sales

The purpose of the interactive analogy is twofold: to capture your prospect's imagination, and to get your prospect to participate in your analogy. If you succeed in getting your prospect's cooperation, you'll dramatically improve your closing ratio.

Here is how it works: First, you describe a simple problem to your prospect and ask for an obvious solution. Next, you point out that that solution is very similar to the one you are proposing for closing the sale.

Master sales closers call this technique the *similar situation close*.

On the following pages you will find five effective closes that can easily be customized to any field of selling.

How the Speeding-Car Analogy Can Get Your Buyer to Act

Mr. Jones, let me ask you a question. If you were standing on the sidewalk and there were two cars of the same make and style, one was parked, and the other was speeding down the street at 40 miles an hour, which car would catch your attention?

[Wait for answer.]

Of course, the moving one, because what draws our attention is action. Look at the most successful people in this world—they got where they are because they took action.

We are in a similar situation here. Let's get moving on this proposal today so that you can help your company travel on the road to success.

How the *Titanic* Analogy Can Sell Superior Quality

Mrs. Brown, do you know why so many people who traveled on the *Titanic* died?

[Wait for answer. She may tell you that the ship ran into an iceberg.]

You'll be surprised to know that only a few people died because of the ship's hitting the iceberg. Almost all the people who perished died because the *Titanic* didn't have enough lifeboats.

You see, buying a product such as this one is very much like traveling on an ocean liner. It costs less to own and operate a ship that has fewer lifeboats, and chances are that you'll never need them. But wouldn't you feel safer traveling on a ship that offered you that little extra security?

[Wait for reply.]

That's exactly what we are talking about here. We offer a superior-quality product that will stand up to the toughest use. You may not need this extra quality in your regular operation, but when it comes to a critical situation, you'll enjoy having the extra safety margin. Isn't that what you wanted?

How the Employment Analogy Can Overcome Price Resistance

This close has been developed in the investment business where salespeople sometimes have to persuade prospects to pay a large amount of money up front. To put things in perspective, a few master sales closers compare the investment to an employment contract. Here is how the employment analogy works:

Mr. Smith, let me make this a bit simpler. You are an experienced businessman. Assume that I came to your office and stated, "I want to work for you for $160 a week for the next year. And I will guarantee to make you a profit that far exceeds my salary. Guaranteed, of course, with the exception of acts of God." Mr. Smith, would you hire me?

[Wait for answer.]

I was sure you would. There is a hitch, though—I need these dollars up front to meet all my expenses. However, that salary of $160 times 52, that is $8,320, will guarantee that I work for you. As many hours as it takes, seven days a week if necessary.

And remember, in addition, I am going to employ a competent staff at no extra cost to you. To ensure that I'm capable of fulfilling my promise. Now, if all the pieces of this puzzle fit, then let's go to work. All we need to get started is your social security number. Do you have it committed to memory?

[Change the dollar amounts to fit your closing situation.]

How the Sailboat Analogy Can Save Your Sale from the Budget Ax

Mr. White, I would like to have your opinion on a very similar situation. Let's assume that you and I are in a sailboat, and you are the captain and I am your mate. Let's also assume that we have been caught by a storm, and our sails are about to be blown out. [Pause.]

Would you order me to cut the sails, or would you ask me to saw off the mast?

[Wait for response.]

I believe that you would want me to cut the sails because we will need to rig the mast again when the storm has blown over. Am I correct?

[Wait for response.]

We are in the same boat now, Mr. White. If I were in your position, I would not want to dispose of the most essential part of the budget because if I did, I might not be able to reach my goals. [Pause.]

Don't you agree that it would be safer to trim the sails a little, and to cut some of the less essential items so that you could continue to weather the storm and reach your destination?

How the Iceberg Analogy Can Sell Your Superior Service

Mrs. Williams, I'd like to ask you a very simple question: When you look at an iceberg, do you really see all there is?

[Wait for reply.]

Of course you don't, since about two-thirds of an iceberg is hidden below the surface.

You see, with our product it is very similar. We are looking only at the tip of the iceberg. What you can't see about our product is the part that's most impressive: our service.

We protect your investment by keeping an extensive parts inventory in our warehouse. In addition, our highly trained service engineers will perform preventive maintenance inspections twice a year at your plant.

You will also be pleased to know that these engineers are instructed to automatically install any upgrades so that you will always have the most advanced equipment.

Isn't that what you expect?

Your Own Analogy Close

_____

_____

_____

_____

_____

CHAPTER 10

The Assumptive Close

Never assume that your prospect cannot be closed.

- Assumptive Closes

How the Assumptive Close Works

At a certain point in your sales presentation, you gradually begin to take it for granted that your prospect is going to buy. Although your prospect has not given you a specific, verbal order, you act as if the actual close were just a mere formality designed to confirm the customer's silent agreement. The assumptive close is based on your bold, yet unspoken, claim that your prospect's decision to buy is already history.

This close is a clever psychological ploy that will often overcome a prospect's gradually weakening resistance. Your assumptive attitude will slowly transform the decreasing resistance into increasing acceptance.

The stronger your commitment to act as if the sale is already closed, the more chances you have for closing the sale.

Creating the Assumptive Attitude

Your subconscious mind respects what your conscious mind actively expects.

Master sales closers know that every close originates in the salesperson's mind. The salesperson builds the assumptive attitude long before the actual sales call with a series of simple visualization exercises.

To become a successful closer, you need to invest a few minutes of your time prior to meeting with your prospect.

Visualize your prospect owning, using, and enjoying your product. Many a top sales closer directs a complete mental movie on the screen of his or her mind, instructing the prospect (in the mental movie) to become enthusiastic about the product or service.

Developing Your Own Positive Visualization Exercise

Below is a description of a typical visualization routine employed by a master sales closer selling office machines:

> **We become what we think about.**
> **—Edgar Russell**

I am entering the customer's office; he looks indifferent, but my enthusiastic and friendly attitude brings a smile to his face. Now I ask my opening questions. He responds well. I listen carefully and take notes. I present my product benefits and get his feedback. He smiles when he hears about the time savings. I hand him a written customer testimonial letter and see his eyes light up. He nods when he hears about the lower maintenance cost, and I get him to confirm that the upkeep for this old machine is much too high. He realizes now that the new model will pay for itself. He's eager to have it installed. He agrees that this is a terrific investment. As we talk, I complete the order form and mark an X next to the dotted line. I turn it over to him and say, "This is the best investment decision you have made today!" He smiles, and he is happy to deal with

CHAPTER 10

our firm. I leave the office with the order and his check. I go back to my car feeling confident, successful, and enthusiastic about my call.

Closing a Larger Sale First in Your Mind

A master sales closer in the construction equipment business once asked me: "What makes you think that you can close the sale in your customer's office when you can't close the sale first in your own mind?" He strongly believed in the power of visualization.

He directed detailed mental movies before each sales call. He went over every single step and played several versions of the closing process.

The same technique can produce astonishing results when you try to sell more than one product to the same customer. Tom Hopkins, a master sales champion in real estate, once told me, "When you sell bananas, you sell them in bunches."

The Silent Assumptive Close

A few years ago, I spent some time in the Midwest with a master sales closer who sold storage buildings to farmers. He had perfected a silent variation of the assumptive close. On one particular day, we made two sales calls. Each time he simply put the sales agreement in front of the prospect and began his presentation. During the closing phase he drew a floor plan of the proposed building and sketched in the doors, skylights, and windows, asking his prospect to help him find just the right position. When he completed the drawing, he said, "Yep, that's exactly what we'll do for you, Jim." Then he silently handed a pen to the former and pointed his index finger to the signature line with a faint smile. I noticed he carefully avoided looking into the customer's eyes as he handed over the pen. To my amazement, both prospects signed without hesitation. They almost appeared hypnotized by this silent master sales closer.

> **After you've closed the sale, close your briefcase, thank your prospect, and leave.**

After we left the second prospect, he told me, "There are two closing ratios; one is in my mind, the other one is in reality. If I see myself closing every sale, I will succeed in closing two out of three prospects. If I see myself closing only two out of three, then my real ratio drops to one out of three."

I asked him why he avoided looking into the prospect's eyes during the close, and he replied, "When I use the silent, assumptive close, I want action, not a staring contest."

This sales rep was a professional—he had guts and audacity.

Attitudes Cannot Replace Skills!

Although the assumptive close appears to work like magic, the real secret to success with the assumptive close has nothing to do with magic. To display an assumptive attitude helps only if you have built a solid foundation for your sale. This means that you have qualified your prospect, understood the dominant buying motives, presented your product convincingly, and handled your customer's concerns like a professional. If you have managed every step of your sale properly, closing will be a foregone conclusion.

> **If you ask for twice as much business as you expect, you often get it.**

A Dutch sales trainer who visited this country during a consulting assignment shared an appropriate analogy with me as we were driving to a customer in his rented Lincoln Continental. He said, "If you have learned how to set the cruise control in this car but haven't yet learned how to drive, then the knowledge of the cruise control won't do you any good. It's the same with the assumptive close. If you haven't mastered the steps of the sale first, the assumptive close is useless."

Summary of Steps to Prepare Yourself for the Assumptive Close

1. Visualize your customer accepting your proposal. Remember that if you can't close the sale in your mind, you won't be able to close the sale in your customer's office.

2. Take the customer's decision to buy for granted. Act as if the sale were a foregone conclusion.

3. Ask your final, assumptive closing question.

Assumptive Closes

1. I took the liberty of completing this paperwork for you. All we need to do is initial this agreement here.

2. Aren't you glad that we've found a solution to your productivity problem?

3. This has been a great meeting, and I am glad we were able to help you. Can you help me with the spelling of your last name? [Begin writing the order.]

4. I am pleased that you recognize the value of quality. I'd like to congratulate you on making the decision to go with us. Please okay both copies.

5. We seem to be in agreement on all major points. When would you like us to begin production?

6. It sounds as if we have addressed all your concerns to your satisfaction. I would like to compliment you on your good taste. I guess that we should put this down on paper now.

7. This has been a most enjoyable meeting, and we look forward to serving your needs for many years to come. Let's review the details of your initial order.

8. I am glad that you made the decision to go with this model because it is so much more economical. Would you feel comfortable with a deposit in the area of $500?

9. Here is your passport to satisfaction. [Hand over contract.] Would you please put your stamp of approval on it?

10. Congratulations. You've made a very wise decision.

11. _____
_____
_____

12. _____
_____
_____

CHAPTER 11

The Negotiation Close

How to arrive at a win-win situation for everyone.

- Negotiating to Remove the Obstacle to the Close
- Negotiating a Creative Compromise
- Negotiating For Better Cooperation
- Negotiating the Decision to Buy
- Negotiating the Close in Exchange For Information

Every sale is a negotiation. Most sales negotiations focus on one major theme: value. Customers will always demand more value. In their quest for more value, prospects will often resort to unfair tactics and put heavy pressure on the sales-person.

> **"Knowledge is power" only in a negotiation where information is not shared by both sides.**

Master sales closers know that the purpose of a good sales negotiation is not to haggle over who gets the larger slice of pie, but to find ways to make more pies for everyone.

Here are five factors to help you reach that goal:

1.　Your Attitude

Tell your client that you appreciate the opportunity of earning his or her business. Also, let it be known that it is important to you to create a win-win situation. Express your need for an agreement that lasts.

2.　Your Game Plan

Salespeople who have little experience in creating a methodology for dealing with problems tend to think that the best they can do is to find one ideal solution for the customer's problem. Master sales closers create several different solutions and actively ask their customers to participate in the design of these solutions.

3.   Your Ability to Be Fair
and to Be Tough

Customers respect you when you are fair with them, but they respect you even more if you are tough enough to insist that they be fair too.

4.   Your Feeling of Power

The worst negotiations are the ones where we feel that we are at a disadvantage. What's even worse is that many salespeople tend to ignore these feelings simply because they don't know what to do about them.

Watch for telltale signs such as negative self-talk: "I can't sell this type," or "I can't deal with these high-level people," or "I can't possibly close a deal that is 10 times larger than the highest sale I ever made."

As soon as you become aware of these self-defeating internal messages, you need to stop whatever you are doing and actively work on dissolving your "I can't" predictions.

The best way to do this is to make a list of your sources of power such as the power of expertise, the power of satisfied customers, the power of your track record, the power of availability, the power of a high-quality product, the power of a solid support team, or the power of a competitive price.

Remember that people respect what you value. Nobody can make you feel inferior without your consent. Don't let them —get 'em.

5. Your Negotiation Rules

On the following pages you will find major negotiation rules that can lead your sale to a close.

> **The type of attitude you project determines the type of attitude you are going to get.**

1. Often a sale won't come to a close because the salesperson is avoiding the need to address the obstacle to the sale in a straight and unreserved manner. Sidestep this trap by isolating the obstacle.

2. Good negotiators develop many alternatives. The famous trial lawyer F. Lee Bailey prepared as many as 50 different defense strategies before he appeared in court.

3. Avoid ego clashes. As a master sales closer, you want to win a sale, not an ego contest. Many times the best solution for better cooperation is to leave your ego at the door.

4. Many closing situations involve high emotions. If your prospect appears nervous or anxious, try to be calm, confident, and patient. A confident salesperson closes more sales.

5. Develop agreements that are good for you and good for the prospect. One-sided agreements don't last. Good sales closers develop long-term, win-win relationships.

CHAPTER 11

Negotiating to Remove the Obstacle to the Close

1. You know that we would appreciate the opportunity to have you as a customer. Could you tell me what we need to do to earn your business?

2. What kind of evidence do you need to have in order for you to be completely satisfied with this purchase?

3. Is price the only reason that prevents you from going ahead with this today?

4. What other hurdles do we need to think about besides the critical issue of financing?

5. _____

_____

_____

6. _____

_____

_____

Negotiating a Creative Compromise

1. If I can get my manager to approve the extended payment terms, will you go ahead with this plan today?

2. What if I could find a way to get you the longer warranty and include the service contract in this deal? Would you be willing to sign the order now?

3. Let's see if we can work this out so we can get you what you want today. Are you saying that if we meet your needs for the lower deposit and give you $300 more on your trade, we have a deal?

4. Just suppose that I can find a way to have this delivered by Friday. Can you find a way to send me your purchase order overnight?

5. _____

_____

_____

6. _____

_____

_____

Negotiating for Better Cooperation

1. Mr. Smith, if you were in my situation, what would you do to get your business?

2. I have never had the opportunity to sell anything to you, yet I've made many calls on your account. Could you tell me what I am doing wrong? What do I need to change or do differently?

3. If I were working for you, would you be able to give me any hints on how to close this deal?

4. If you were my sales manager, what strategy would you recommend for meeting the expectations of your board of directors?

5. _____

_____

_____

6. _____

_____

_____

Negotiating the Decision to Buy

1. Do you know the difference between dreams and goals? [Wait for answer.] Well, I read somewhere that a goal is a dream with a deadline. Why don't you sign this now so that we can set a deadline for making this dream come true?

2. If you are prepared to make a decision on the color today, I am prepared to guarantee you completion by the end of this month.

3. Mr. Brown, you are a shrewd businessman. You know that time equals money. You know better than I that if you wait three months, you may have to pay a lot more for the same product. I believe that the only question you need to ask yourself is: How much can I save during the next three months by having this product installed today? Don't you think that it is to your advantage to order now?

4. I don't know if you are aware of this; however, the terms of this sale expire on the 10th. I have already received the new price list. It does reflect an 8 percent increase over what we have quoted you. Do you prefer to increase your investment commitment by 8 percent, or do you prefer to increase your savings by 8 percent?

5. _____

_____

_____

6. _____

_____

_____

Negotiating the Close in Exchange for Information

1. *Customer*: Does this come in red?

Salesperson: Would you buy it if we had one in red?

2. *Customer*: Can you get automatic controls on this machine?

Salesperson: If we could get automatic controls for you, would you order this machine today?

3. *Customer*: Can you ship this by the end of the month?

Salesperson: I will check for you. Can I assume that we have a deal if we can get it to you by then?

4. *Customer*: Can you give me an extra $300 discount?

Salesperson: I don't know if my manager will approve it. If I can get her to say "yes," would you be prepared to write a deposit check today?

5. _____

_____

_____

6. _____

_____

_____

CHAPTER 12

The Direct Close

Good prospects never reject good salesmanship.

- Ask For the Order in No Uncertain Terms

The **C** in the Word *Close*

A newly hired advertising salesperson felt that the first three months on the job were the toughest for her. She had received no formal sales training and had been instructed simply to make calls.

Surprised that nobody would buy from her, she talked to a stockbroker friend and told him about her situation. His first question was, "What is your closing ratio?" She asked in return, "What in the world are you talking about?" She had never heard of "closing techniques" or "closing ratios" and thought that if you did a good job in presenting your opportunity, the prospect would buy automatically.

He suggested ending each of her sales presentations by asking directly for the order. She followed this simple advice, and her order book began to fill up and her confidence increased 100 percent.

Zig Ziglar, a master sales closer and bestselling author explains in his lectures: "The letter *c* in the word *close* stands for 'confidence.' Without the letter *c*, without that confidence, the word would read *lose*."

The direct close is the easiest close to develop, and even though it requires little preparation, many salespeople hesitate to use it consistently on every call.

If not asking for the order amounts to losing the sale, why is it that so many salespeople fail to use a direct close?

> **If you expect success, you will get success!**

The answer can be found in one simple word: *attitude*. They tend to proceed on the theory that their prospects usually know what their own best interests are. They don't. In fact, nobody always does.

The majority of our prospects are going contrary to their best interests every single day. Their preoccupation with the daily problems of business causes them to wear blinders that prevent them from recognizing the value of a new opportunity.

Many salespeople say in their defense for not closing, "I don't want to force my business on him. If he doesn't want to buy, there is nothing that I can do." They overlook that their visit amounts to nothing more than a warm-up call for their competitor. They fail to analyze their sales presentations and lack the courage to admit that their approach and their attitude could benefit from a little improvement.

It is a curious phenomenon that these salespeople don't realize that they too act against their own best interests every single day. They have a hunch about what would be good for them; however, they are not acting on their hunches.

A firm commitment to using the direct close on every sales call is the best cure for losing sales. If you ask for the order and get it, you win. If you ask for the order and don't get it, chances are that you will win too. Your customer will tell you where you failed to convince him or her, and you will have a chance to correct your approach on the next call. Direct closes always help your direction in selling.

The Direct Close Will Help You Find Your Way to Success

The first man ever to set foot on the North Pole was Robert E. Peary. He started his eventful voyage in the summer of 1908 from

New York harbor on a day when more than 70 people suffered from heat stroke. Once he arrived in the polar region, he spent weeks on end fighting the bone-chilling Arctic double-digit sub-zero weather. Many times the temperature was so low that it would not register on his instruments. At the end of each day, the team of Americans and Eskimos spent two to three hours building an igloo to escape the deadly windchill during the night. The next morning they would melt some ice, brew tea, eat breakfast, leave the igloo, and cover another 5 or 10 miles across the awesome and desolate polar landscape. Then another igloo was built and another night spent in uncertainty. The outcome of the expedition was doubtful, especially since dozens of explorers had lost their lives in previous attempts to reach the North Pole.

Yet Commander Peary inspired his team with one single straightforward sentence: "We'll find a way, or make one."

Peary took a direct approach to every single problem they faced on their trip. His attitude to life was, "Solve a problem before it wears you down."

Finally, on April 6, 1909, he became the first man on Earth to set foot on the North Pole. His success story is printed in almost every history book in the world.

Robert Peary's story has several lessons for finding or making your way to becoming a master sales closer.

1.   *Every buyer's mind is inherently cold to the idea of buying your product.* If you refuse to directly explore this cold territory, you'll fail.

2. *Every achievement is preceded by a shared dream.* Most people dream alone. Peary shared his dream and received the support he needed to make his dream come true. Be direct about your dreams; tell people what you want and why you want it. Ask for the order without ifs and buts. You want the sale because it will be beneficial to your customer, period.

3. *When obstacles come your way, go and find a new way.* If you can't find a new way, go ahead and make one. Use every ounce of your strength in a straightforward way and you will reach your destination.

4. *When we are young, we tend to ignore our limitations. When we get older, we tend to ignore our possibilities.* Robert E. Peary was 53 years old when he reached the North

Pole. How old are you today, and what are you avoiding because you think you are too old or too young?

5. *There is no substitute for courage.* Think of your next call right now. Imagine for a second how much courage it took Peary to reach the North Pole. If the amount of courage it took Peary to reach the North Pole were equal to 100 percent, what amount of courage would it take you to use the direct close on your next call?

Ask For the Order in No Uncertain Terms

1. There is only one question left: When would you like us to deliver this to you?

2. Shall we reserve one for you today?

3. Would you like to drive this one home today?

4. Do I have your permission to go ahead with this schedule?

5. Does this agreement suit your expectations?

6. Can we go ahead and sign this now?

7. May I suggest that we write this up now?

8. I would like to have your autograph here.

9. Congratulations, we can start celebrating.

10. Would you please write a deposit check while I complete the paperwork?

11. May I have your signature now?

12. Can we go ahead and schedule production for next month?

13. Do I understand you correctly that we have your business?

14. Would you please write your name on this application?

15. I believe that we have just concluded a very successful deal. Let me shake your hand and thank you for your business!

16. Mr. Brown, you are a tough negotiator. Thank you for giving me the opportunity to serve you. When would you like us to deliver this?

17. Shall we send it out today?

18. Are you certain that one is enough? It will take me just as short a time to write this order for two.

19. Besides this order, is there anything else I can help you with today?

20. Could you please give me your purchase order so that I can send you an invoice?

21. Do you have any preference as to where we should ship this first lot?

22. Could you please make the check out to Brown, Inc.? We are glad to have your business.

23. Well, I guess that wraps it up. Your heart is set on this one. Would you like to take it with you?

24. Okay, that's a deal! Congratulations!

25. Would you please sign this application for me now?

26. _____

_____

_____

27. _____

_____

_____

> **If your dreams
> don't come true,
> you may be
> oversleeping.**

CHAPTER
13

The Suggestion
Close

Just one simple idea can close a sale.

- All It Takes Is One Good Suggestion to Close a Sale

All It Takes Is One Good Suggestion to Close a Sale

Master sales closers know that a million-dollar sale often hinges on one simple idea to tilt the scales in their favor.

The following suggestion closes have been responsible for sales in excess of $10 million. These effective closes have been collected from master closers in the United States, England, France, Germany, Italy, and my native country, Austria.

The "Hunch" Close

Salesperson: Do you believe in hunches?
Customer: Yes.
Salesperson: So do I. And I had a hunch just this morning that you were going to buy from me today.

The "Trust-Me" Close

Mr. Prospect, I was brought up the old-fashioned way: My parents taught me that a person's word is the most important thing he or she has. If a person's word means nothing, then that person means nothing. My word is my bond, and when I give my word, you can take it to the bank. I am giving you my word that you are not only going to get the very best product but also the very best service because I will personally see to it that your needs will be met 100 percent. Just give me 1 percent of your confidence and sign this order now, and I'll earn the other 99 percent.

The "Image" Close

Mr. Norton, just imagine a few months from now. You walk down to your pond. It's a beautiful, sunny day in the fall. Your trees have turned into bright colors, a few snow geese are flying overhead, and you feel the fresh air in your lungs. You are thinking about today and say to yourself, "What a great decision I made to pick this spot for our home."

The "Dollar-Bill" Close

Salesperson: Mrs. Smith, do you have a dollar bill?

Customer: Yes, why?

Salesperson: Could you hand me a dollar bill just for one moment, please?

Customer: All right, here it is.

Salesperson: [Takes dollar bill.] How would you feel if I came to your office every hour and asked you to give me a dollar bill?

Customer: I would not like it a bit.

Salesperson: You see, the machine we have been discussing will save you exactly $1 in maintenance cost every hour of operation. This is your money [gives back dollar bill], and you get to keep it. In fact, by going with this machine, you will save $8 a day,

$40 a week, and $2,000 a year and every year thereafter. Isn't that the best reason to order this machine today?

The "Give-In" Close

Okay, you win. I don't know how I am going to convince my sales manager to accept this order, but go ahead and sign it now, then write a deposit check, and I will get him at his weakest moment first thing tomorrow and get it approved for you.

The "Balance Sheet" Close

Salesperson: Mrs. Dunlap, when you open your financial statement, you always look to see how both sides balance each other. If the balance is in your favor, then you have a profit. Am I correct?

Customer: Yes, why?

Salesperson: Well, we are in a similar situation here. On one hand, we have an investment of $4,000, and on the other hand, you have a computer that will solve your billing problems, handle your extra inventory situation, and satisfy your word processing needs. This means that the value on the credit side will quickly exceed the original investment, and you'll show a healthy profit in less than one year. You see that this is not a luxury item but a necessary investment, and a paying one.

The "Cost" Close

It is not what this service costs that you should consider but how much money it would cost each year to be without it.

The "Cork" Close

You know that there are two values to every investment. One is what is costs, the other is what it saves. For example, cork costs about 25 cents per pound, but if you were drowning 10 yards from shore, its value would not be what you pay for cork but what cork saves you. Let's not confuse the two values by looking only at what you invest.

The "Doctor" Close

Salesperson: Mrs. Brown, if your husband were sick, would you wait another day to call a doctor? Would you put it off until he got better?

Customer: No, why?

Salesperson: I believe that you would get the best doctor as quickly as you could. You see, we are in a similar situation here. Your department has a little cold. Productivity has suffered, and people are unhappy with your copy machine. Don't let them suffer when a simple purchase order with your signature will take care of the problem.

The "Integrity" Close

Mrs. Smith, if you have any doubt in your mind about signing this order, please tell me so now because I would not feel right about selling this product to someone who does not believe that it will be beneficial.

The "Last-Chance" Close

Mr. Customer, you have studied my proposal very carefully, and you have agreed that it meets your needs. We have only one unit left in our inventory. I know that next week you will be glad you made the decision to buy today. I don't think you want this one to go to another customer this afternoon. Do you?

The "Other-Side-of-the-Coin" Close

Let me put it another way: This product is going to cost you a little more money than you figured. That happens to everybody. However, on the other side of the coin, you will get a product that will help you make a lot more profit than you ever thought possible.

The "Only-Question" Close

Mr. Roberts, the only question you need to ask yourself is: How many extra sales do I need to justify this investment?

The "Millionaire" Close

Mr. Prospect, if you were a millionaire living in a big house on the ocean, you would be able to buy a cheap product because you would have enough money to buy a new one each time it breaks down. But unfortunately we are not in that situation. You can't afford to take a chance on something cheap, because your new business depends on the proper functioning of this equipment.

The "Similar-Comment" Close

I understand how you feel. Many customers have made similar comments prior to making this investment. However, they have found out that this product really pays for itself. But I am not asking you to believe what others say, or what we say about this. I'd like you to see it for yourself. Will you be willing to let us arrange a demonstration?

The "Three-Question" Close

Salesperson: Mr. Smith, there are only three questions that we need to look at. First, does this product meet your needs? I believe that the answer is "yes." Am I correct?

Customer:	Yes.
Salesperson:	The second question is, will it cost you money by not having it? I believe we have answered that question before, right?
Customer:	Yes.
Salesperson:	The third question is, can you afford to buy it? Can you?
Customer:	Yes.
Salesperson:	Then it seems that you do want to go ahead with this?
Customer:	Yes.

The "You-Can't-Quite-Afford-It" Close

Mr. Customer, you know, sometimes the best time to buy is when you feel that you just can't quite afford it.

The "Nonnegotiable-Check" Close

This close requires a little advance preparation. First, calculate the total savings of your product over the next five years. Second, write a real company check for that amount, sign the check, and write "not negotiable" above your signature. Third, write this note with your check: "Dear Mr. Smith, this check represents five years' worth of savings from the extra value in the new product we will discuss next week. Can you afford not to consider this investment? During our discussion I will show you how to make this check negotiable. Thank you."

Fourth, when you meet your prospect, simply explain: "Mr. Smith, making this investment will be almost like opening a savings account in your company's name. At the end of five years you will be able to write yourself a check for the exact same amount I wrote on the check I sent you last week. I believe that you want to turn these dollar savings into hard cash. Do you agree?"

Your Own Suggestion Close

_____

_____

_____

_____

_____

CHAPTER 14

Your Closing Words

How to maximize the impact of your closing words.

- Use Reassuring Words to Eliminate the Fear of Buying
- Use Finesse When You Ask For the Order

Your Closing Words Are Like Diamonds

Sometimes salespeople express themselves clumsily. Their words do not communicate the exact thoughts they want to express. Their speech patterns may reveal sloppy thinking, poor preparation, or lack of confidence.

Carefully select your closing words as if you were choosing an expensive diamond. Master sales closers, like master diamond cutters, spend many hours polishing and refining their closes until they achieve the highest grade, "flawless." A flawless diamond can be worth a fortune.

Effective closes are worth far more than flawless diamonds. While a perfect diamond can double its original value in a few years, an effective close can double its value in a few days.

To achieve better clarity and improved sound and to increase your value as a closer, polish your closing words.

For example, a preowned car seems more valuable than a used car. Footwear is higher priced than shoes. A journal is more expensive than a magazine. A business that refers to its clientele is expected to charge more than one that has ordinary customers.

One excellent way to sharpen your closing words is to select a series of words with similar meanings. For example, instead of saying "new information," you can pick similar words like: *up-to-the minute data, facts as fresh as the morning dew, a hot inside story,*

> **Nothing is more powerful than words. The linking of powerful arguments and noble thoughts forms a chain that nothing can break.**
> **—Anatole France**

a fresh scoop, an amazing tip, a revolutionary discovery, an advanced intelligence report, or *a brand-new message.*

How to Pack Meaning into Your Close

You can't be convincing if your words are confusing!

Studies have shown that the greater your capacity to use the right words, the higher your closing ratio.

Charles Roth, a master sales closer, once said, "A salesperson trying to get by with a few hundred words is like an artisan trying to do all the tasks that need to be done in building a house with a pocket knife."

But quantity alone doesn't count. Quality does. The quality of your closing words can be judged by their clarity. Dr. Norman Vincent Peale once defined *salesmanship* as "a process of persuasion whereby another individual is induced to walk the road of agreement with you."

Your words should illuminate your prospect's mental path from the desire stage to the decision stage. The more clearly you express yourself, the easier it will become for your prospect to walk with you on the road of agreement. Clarity demands that you pack more meaning into fewer words.

Samuel Knox, a leading sales trainer, once said, "In closing, there are meaty words and watery words. Meaty words inject a burst of meaning into a single phrase. Watery words are shapeless ghosts of thoughts, and their meaning is lost no matter how well the words are spoken."

> **Words cut more than swords.**
> **—Japanese Proverb**

CHAPTER 14

Sales psychologists have identified six groups of "watery words" that can kill your close.

Eliminate Watery Words from Your Close

1. *Groping words:*

- "What I am trying to tell you ..."
- "In other words ..."
- "The point I am trying to make is ..."

2. *Trite phrases:*

- "Let me be perfectly honest with you ..."
- "I can say this without any fear of contradiction ..."
- "Obviously this idea needs no introduction ..."

3. *Repetitious language:*

- "Let me say this again ..."
- "As I just said to you ..."
- "I don't want to be redundant, but ..."

4. *Weasel words*:

- "You understand, this is just my opinion..."
- "You may disagree with this statement..."
- "I may be 100 percent wrong..."

5. *Superlative declarations*:

- "This is positively the crème de la crème model. You can't find anything equal to this anywhere."
- "This is unquestionably an unparalleled quality, and it is absolutely and positively the best."

6. *Negative subject matter*:

- Don't talk about your health, your political views, your personal problems, your religious beliefs, or your sexual preferences.
- Don't interrupt, don't contradict, don't change the subject. Your objective is to close the sale. Your chances of getting the order will always hinge on your choice of words.

Put More Closing Power into Your Voice

Two salespeople may use the same close on the same type of prospect. One gets the order and the other does not. Yet, word for word, they used the same close. Why did one succeed where the other failed?

> **No farmer ever plowed a field by turning it over in his mind.**

Chances are that one salesperson used the correct tone of voice, the right kind of emphasis, the appropriate degree of enthusiasm, while he skillfully matched his prospect's rate of speech.

Oliver Wendell Holmes once wrote, "A word is not a crystal, transparent and unchanged; it is the skin of a living thought that may vary greatly in color and content according to the circumstances in which it is used."

Exercise Your Voice to Increase Your Closing Fitness

To perk up your closing energy, practice your closing words in front of a full-length mirror or a video camera. Repeat each close at least six times. First, close with enthusiasm. Second, close with a lower-pitched voice. Third, close with very relaxed nonverbal expressions. Fourth, close with a smile. Fifth, close with steady eye contact. Sixth, close with your most effective cadence.

Rate yourself on a scale from 1 to 10 after each practice close. Learn from each rehearsal. Study your timing and your pauses.

Drop what doesn't work for you. Here are seven tips for packing more closing power into your voice:

1. A lower-pitched voice is always more pleasant than a high-pitched voice; use your lowest pitch when you ask for the order.

2. Pauses are terrific attention-getters.

3. A monotone voice is good only for funerals.

4. A soft voice indicates uncertainty.

5. Loud voices are telltale signs of high-pressure selling.

6. Allow natural gestures to accent your voice.

7. Never stare at your customer when you ask for the order.

Add Power Words to Your Closes

More than 50 years ago, Dale Carnegie, the author of *How to Win Friends and Influence People*, taught his students, "If you remember my name, you pay me a subtle compliment; you indicate that I have made an impression on you."

Your prospect's name is one of the most powerful closing tools for the obvious reason that all of us are more interested in ourselves than we are in anyone else.

Repeat your prospect's name several times during your sales call. Connect your prospect's name with major benefit statements like, "This automatic dialing feature,

> **Your prospect's name is a great closing.**

Jim, will save you a lot of time," or "Our warranty is designed to give you peace of mind, Susan." Your prospect will not know that you are using a powerful psychological strategy called *positive pairing*. In advertising, a celebrity holding a box of cereal is a typical application of positive pairing.

If you have connected your prospect's name with three or four prominent product benefits, your customer will begin to expect to hear something positive when you merely mention his or her name. When you approach your close, remember to use your prospect's name. Chances are that the sound of his or her name will again evoke positive feelings. By using this little-known secret of master sales closers, you will quickly close more sales than you ever thought possible.

Don't Stumble Over the All-Important Subject of Price

All prospects are sensitive to how the price is presented to them. Below is a typical listing of negative and positive ways to deal with price issues during the closing phase:

Negative Words	Positive Words
• This costs two thousand three hundred dollars.	• This is only twenty-three hundred.
• Your down payment…	• Your initial investment…
• Your monthly payment…	• Your monthly investment…
• You can pay the purchase price over a series of months.	• We would be happy to divide this investment into small monthly shares.
• How much would you like to pay us every month?	• What monthly investment would you feel comfortable with?
• We'll charge you 2 points above the prime rate.	• Your rate will be only prime plus 2.
• We'll take off sixty-seven hundred to trade in your used car.	• We are offering you six thousand seven hundred dollars to trade your existing model.

Use Reassuring Words to Eliminate the Fear of Buying

Your words can have a powerful effect on your prospect's emotions. A soothing voice and carefully chosen words can quickly calm last-minute buying fears. The following phrases have been collected from master sales closers who used them to relax their customers. When you use any of the phrases below, be sure to look into your customer's eyes and avoid blinking:

1. You will be pleased to become the owner of this high-quality product.

2. I am confident that your boss (your spouse, your partner, or other person) will enjoy this product just as much as you do.

3. You and I know that the worst feeling is to pay dearly for something that isn't fun to own. You are getting something that you will be proud of, which makes it easier to invest in.

4. Just last week I had a customer tell me, "Jim, I have never spent so much money in my life, and I never had more fun doing it."

5. Your savings in operating costs alone justify the investment. I know that you will be very happy you made this decision.

6. Your headquarters will admire your initiative in going ahead with this profitable plan.

7. I am convinced that once you have used this product for one week, you will not want to sell it back to me for twice its cost.

8. _____
_____
_____

9. _____
_____
_____

Use Finesse When You Ask For the Order

Closing demands shrewdness and sensitivity. Just as pharmacists sugarcoat their pills, dip your closing words in honey. It works.

1. Would you please okay this for me?

2. Can we go ahead and confirm our understanding?

3. I'd like to have you initial our agreement.

4. Would you please take a moment to check the details of this bargain?

5. Could we just take a minute to confirm this arrangement?

6. Is it all right with you to seal this deal now?

7. Can I get you to double-check the terms?

8. I'd appreciate your endorsement right here.

9. Please validate this application.

10. Please write your name here so that we can give our manufacturing department the green light.

11. To get the ball rolling, we need to have your initials.

12. If we can get your confirmation now, we'll begin working on your project next Monday.

13. I'd like you to take a moment and double-check your address here and then write your full name down below.

14. _____

_____

_____

15. _____

_____

_____

CHAPTER 15

Timing Your Close

How to decide when to close.

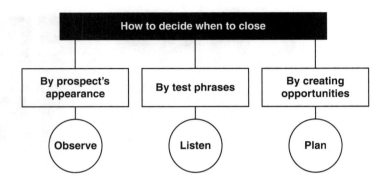

Your Prospect's Appearance Will
Tell You When to Close

Dr. Albert Mehrabian, a noted specialist in nonverbal communication, found that our feelings and attitudes are communicated 7 percent with words, 38 percent via tone of voice, and 55 percent nonverbally.

During every sales call, hundreds of nonverbal signals are exchanged. Although these signals are clearly visible, very few salespeople make a concentrated effort to study their meaning.

Although isolated gestures like crossed arms may have no particular meaning to your selling strategy, a group or cluster of gestures can alert you to an important shift in your customer's attitude.

Master sales closers have identified a series of nonverbal signals that prospects only communicate when their interest is at a peak level.

> **All the treasures of the earth cannot bring back one lost moment.**
> **—French Proverb**

Ten Major Nonverbal Buying Signals

The following changes in your prospect's appearance usually indicate an increased interest in your product or service. When you notice these signals, use a trial close:

> No mortal man can keep a secret. If his lips are silent, he chatters with his fingertips; betrayal oozes out of him at every pore.
> —Sigmund Freud

1. You notice a subtle change in your prospect's facial expressions. The lines begin to relax, and smiles begin to appear.

2. Your prospect leans forward or moves closer to you.

3. Your prospect begins to mirror your positive gestures or postures.

4. You notice an unusual sparkle in your prospect's eyes.

5. Your customer's hands begin to relax; you notice open palms.

6. Your prospect picks up your product (or brochure) and studies it with great interest.

7. Your prospect begins to examine your contract.

8. Your prospect answers your summary statement with repeated head nods.

9. Your prospects exchange approving glances with each other.

10. You notice pleasant sounds like humming or whistling.

When you notice any of these signals, don't hesitate—close!

Your Prospect's Next Question May Be a Closing Signal

There are seven specific types of questions that indicate a strong interest in buying your product. When you hear these high-interest questions, go for the close:

1. *Questions about the terms of the sale.* Your prospect is testing and measuring the total cost of your proposal.

> **Make it a habit to answer high-interest questions with a trial close!**

Question: Is freight included in the price?

Wrong answer: Yes.

Right answer: That depends on how you want us to ship it to you. Would you prefer overnight, which is $45 extra, or do you want standard UPS, which is only $5? How would you like us to ship it?

2. *Interest in a specific product.* Your prospect is trying to match the product to fit his or her particular needs.

Question: Do you have it in light green?

Wrong answer: Yes.

Right answer: Would you like it in light green?

3. *Concerns about warranties.* Your prospect is considering a worst-case scenario.

Question: If this car breaks down, will you give me a loaner while it is in the shop?

Wrong answer: Yes.

Right answer: If I could get my manager to approve a loaner for you in that case, do we have a deal?

4. *Requests for a specific demonstration.* Your prospect needs physical proof that your product will perform to specification.

Question: Could you show me if this crane will lift a 600-pound load at 28-foot reach? *Wrong answer*: No problem. I'll ask our operator to show you that it can be done. *Right answer*: Is it important to you that this machine will do that? [Wait for "yes" response.] If our machine can lift this load at that distance, will you buy it?

5. *Questions about delivery.* Your prospect is mentally taking ownership of your product. *Question*: How soon can I have this delivered? *Wrong answer*: In about two weeks. *Right answer*: How soon would you like to have this delivered?

6. *Questions about references.* Your prospect has decided to verify your information. *Question*: Do you know anybody who has bought that type of copier with this special collator?

Wrong answer: Yes, I can give you three names.

Right answer: Let's see ... if I can provide you with three customer names and if all three will confirm that our copier can do this type of work, will you go ahead with this plan?

7. *A question that backtracks to an earlier point.* Your prospect is refocusing on a final detail.

Question: Can you explain again how the service contract works?

Wrong answer: Of course ...

Right answer: It sounds like you are seriously interested in this equipment. Are there any other questions besides the service contract?

Your Prospect's Positive Comments
Are Buying Signals

Master sales closers are skilled in eliciting positive reactions from their prospect. Once these positive comments are expressed, a trial close is the only logical response. Here are a few examples of how you can transform positive comments into a close:

1. *Customer*: That's a great idea!

  Salesperson: I am glad you agree. Would you like to order now?

2. *Customer*: I can see how this would save time.

  Salesperson: You are very perceptive. Is it important to you to save time in your business?

3. *Customer*: This machine is surprisingly fast.

  Salesperson: Yes, it is. How fast do you want us to deliver one?

4. *Customer*: This is not very expensive.
Salesperson: I agree. It is so economical that you can't afford not to get one. Do you agree?

5. *Customer*: That is a nice looking car.
Salesperson: I can see you driving it home today. Can you?

6. *Customer*: This computer is the most powerful I've ever seen.
Salesperson: Yes, you are looking at the most powerful model. I assume that this is the one you want.

How to Create More Closing Opportunities

Master sales closers are prepared to close the sale at any moment during the sales call. Here are five strategic opportunities for closing your sale:

1. *Begin your sale with a close.* Mr. Prospect, the purpose of my call is to gain your confidence in this new product. If I succeed in convincing you of its value, would you consider buying it today?

2. *Start your sales presentation with your close.* If I could show you a way that it could solve your productivity problems, would you consider investing in this product?

3. *Use a trial close after each benefit statement.* As you can see, this high-speed machine will handle your increased volume and cut your labor cost by 45 percent. Isn't that alone worth the investment?

4. *Close after you have completed your demonstration.* Now that you have seen how this feature works, do you agree that this alone justifies doing business with us?

5. *Close after you have handled an objection.* A cheap product is like a boat with a steady leak in the bottom. It will do the job for a while, but it won't hold you for long. You don't want to risk taking a bath, do you?

CHAPTER 16

Closing Attitudes

Persistence will lead to success.

The Most Significant Instrument for Influencing Your Customer Is Called "Attitude"

"I wish it were possible to impress upon the minds of the young the tremendous power which the right attitude has to bring about success." These words, written over 80 years ago by Orison Swett Marden, are still true today.

Dr. Sidney Bremer, a renowned author and researcher, once said, "The one who holds the negative, despondent, fearful, anxious or sorrowful attitude, whether he intends it or not, is, by the law of suggestion, creating forces that make people sad, discouraged, fearful, and anxious."

Master sales closers realize that they cannot control their customers; they can only influence their customers' attitudes. The best means for influencing a customer's attitude is by controlling your own attitude.

Here are three essential attitudes that can multiply your closing power:

1. The attitude of persistence

2. The attitude of sincere enthusiasm

3. The attitude of exceptional value

On the following pages you will find specific action steps to create, enhance, and maintain these important closing attitudes for increased sales.

The Attitude of Persistence

Master sales closers choose to endure in spite of difficulties. They ask closing questions in the face of customer objections; they justly interpret a "no" as a request for additional information; they are committed to asking for the order as many times as it takes to get it.

Few companies set specific guidelines for salespeople regarding how many attempts should be made to close a sale.

However, in the life insurance industry, many companies suggest that their salespeople make at least three attempts to close the sale during every organized presentation.

> **Without standards for persistence, salespeople will go the path of least resistance.**

A survey of closing attempts conducted at Notre Dame University found that

- 46 percent asked for the order once and then quit.
- 24 percent asked for the order twice and then quit.
- 14 percent asked for the order only three times.
- 12 percent asked for the order only four times.

Yet the survey showed that 60 percent of the acceptances came on the fifth attempt.

CHAPTER 16

Your Persistence Will Help Your Prospects

One of America's leading master sales closers, James Samuel Knox, said many years ago, "When I am convinced that my proposition is to a prospect's advantage and will make him money, and then fail to urge him to take it, I feel that I am not giving him a square deal. That is the reason I am so persistent."

Seven Reasons Why Persistence Always Benefits Both You and Your Prospect

1.

Your prospects often don't know what their own best interests are. ... You need to persist in educating them until they do understand.

> **Consider the postage stamp: Its usefulness consists of the ability to stick to one thing until it gets there.**

2.

Prospects often appear blind to the things that will help them improve their situation. ... You need to persist in helping them visualize a brighter future.

3. Prospects are reluctant to change.

... You need to point out to them how costly it is not to change, not to have your product, or not to utilize your time-saving and cost-saving services.

4. Although prospects have plenty of desire, they have little resolve.

... You need to persist in identifying the nature of their resistance and help them tear it down.

5. Prospects often have difficulty comparing the many different products objectively.

... You need to persist and explain point by point how and why your product is superior.

6. Don't "warm up" your prospect for your competitor.

... You need to persist in asking for the order. If you don't close, your competitor will.

7. Prospects are often mentally overloaded and not capable of clear thoughts.

... You need to persist, relax your prospects, and patiently start your presentation over again.

When Too Much Persistence Can Hurt You

Master sales closers know when to stop. Just as a carpenter stops hammering a nail after it is all the way in, or a prize fighter stops punching an opponent who is down and out, the professional salesperson stops talking after the sale is closed.

The Attitude of Sincere Enthusiasm—How to Win the Struggle against Inertia

No matter how perfectly constructed a steam locomotive may be, unless the water is heated past the boiling point, the train will not move an inch. Hot water, water at 211 degrees, will not work. The water must exceed the boiling point.

No matter how perfectly trained a salesperson may be, without the steam of enthusiasm, which propels him or her to the close, all sales knowledge is ineffective.

It is the enthusiastic salesperson whose inner system has surpassed the boiling point who keeps the economy moving at a high rate of speed.

How to Create Peak Enthusiasm

You can be enthusiastic and please your customers without overstepping the bounds of good taste. Amateur sales closers tend to have difficulty generating and harnessing the power of enthusiasm. At times they are unenthusiastic without being aware of their negative attitude, and at other times they are overly enthusiastic without realizing that excessive enthusiasm can antagonize a prospect.

Peak enthusiasm is balanced enthusiasm. It is balanced in such a manner that it positively influences the customer's feelings about the salesperson and the purchase.

Is Your Enthusiasm Honest and Sincere?

To be sincere implies an absence of deceit, pretense, or hypocrisy. In other words, you resolve to stick to the simple, unembellished truth.

Master sales closers cultivate an attitude of sincere enthusiasm by reviewing and answering the following questions:

1. Am I totally convinced that my product is the best solution to my prospect's problem?

☐ YES   ☐ NO

CHAPTER 16

2. Am I committed to help my prospect the same way I would help my best friend?
☐ YES   ☐ NO

> **Insincere enthusiasm tends to work against you.**

3. Am I representing my company with the highest level of integrity?
☐ YES   ☐ NO

4. Am I prepared to back up all promises I make to my prospect?
☐ YES   ☐ NO

5. Am I truthful about the statements I make about my products, their performance, and our services?   ☐ YES   ☐ NO

6. Am I prepared to stop selling when I realize that the customer has already signed an order with my competitor?
☐ YES   ☐ NO

7. Am I willing to say "I don't know" when I don't have the answer to a prospect's question? ☐ YES   ☐ NO

If you can't answer all seven questions with an enthusiastic "yes," revise and correct your attitude prior to your next call.

Every Close Begins by Selling Yourself

Before you can sell to anybody, you need to make a secret deal, a commitment to yourself that you will close the sale. Once you have promised yourself to take positive action, you will remove any hesitancy, fear, or doubt from your mind and close the sale.

Many master sales closers use secret chants, songs, or short pep talks to recharge their batteries before the sales call.

Over 65 years ago, a French doctor named Emile Coue became world famous for his positive affirmations. His magic sentence was:

Every day, in every way, I am getting better and better.

He taught people to repeat this sentence 20 times in the morning and 20 times in the evening. According to many reports, this single sentence was responsible for boosting confidence, eliminating fears, and causing seemingly miraculous recoveries from chronic diseases.

Tested Enthusiasm Builders from Master Sales Closers

The following autosuggestive sentences have been used by sales champions in the United States and Europe. Some of these sentences may sound silly. However, they have served their creators well and brought them considerable success.

1. I am cool, calm, and confident, and I will do everything in my power to close this sale.

2. This is a terrific day for closing the sale. I am right, I am resourceful, I am ready.

3. Every day I am getting closing barriers out of my way.

4. Nothing can hold me back from closing more sales and staying in the black.

5. I feel good, I feel fine, I'm getting better at closing all the time.

6. I am the best by any scale because I'll win the toughest sale.

7. Mirror, mirror on the wall, guess who is out to win it all!

The Attitude of Exceptional Value

Selling is an exchange of values. Your prospect will buy when he or she realizes that the value of your product is far greater than the price you are asking.

Master sales closers don't limit themselves to selling the value of the product alone. They always add exceptional value to every sale. There is a limit to how much you can charge for your product. However, there is no limit to how much value you can add to your sales presentation.

> **Remember your ABCs: Always Be Closing.**

Below you will find seven specific ideas on how you can add exceptional value during your next sale:

1. *The value of your company.* Our company has had over 15 years of experience in solving problems such as the one you are dealing with today.

2. *The value of your testimonials.* Here is a list of Fortune 500 companies that have used our services. I'd like to draw your attention to a few of the letters written by satisfied customers.

3. *The value of your service team.* We have 20 service centers across the country, and you will be pleased to know that we have the best service record in the industry.

4. *The value of your professional training.* Every salesperson is required to complete a six-week training program and pass a thorough test before meeting with customers.

5. *The value of your personal sensitivity.* I understand how you feel. You should not have been treated in this manner by our representative. I will make sure that this will not happen again.

6. *The value of your personal commitment.* Here is my home telephone number. Please do not hesitate to use it if you think I can help you.

7. *The value of your dedication.* I see my role as that of an ambassador between you and my company. I will not rest until all of your questions have been answered to your complete satisfaction.

If You Want Your Ship to Come In, You Must Send Out a Fleet

Like streams carry ships, rafts, or tree stumps, thoughts are the carriers of decisions, judgments, and emotions. As with any flowing stream, your prospect's mind never stands still, and one thought is quickly replaced by another. Your job as a salesperson consists of sounding out the carrying capacity of your prospect's mental stream to launch your ships (ideas that communicate exceptional value) and to make sure they'll safely reach your prospect's flagship, *customer satisfaction.*

> **When it's time to sell, slow down.**
> **When it's time to close, seize the moment.**
> **When it's time to follow up, speed.**

© Hisham Bharoocha

About the Author

A dual citizen of both Austria and the United States, Gerhard Gschwandtner is the founder and publisher of *Selling Power*, the leading magazine for sales professionals worldwide, with a circulation of 165,000 subscribers in 67 countries.

He began his career in his native Austria in the sales training and marketing departments of a large construction equipment company. In 1972, he moved to the United States to become the company's North American Sales Training Director, later moving into the position of Marketing Manager.

In 1977, he became an independent sales training consultant, and in 1979 he created an audiovisual sales training course called "The Languages of Selling." Marketed to sales managers at Fortune 500 companies, the course taught nonverbal communication in sales together with professional selling skills.

In 1981, Gerhard launched *Personal Selling Power*, a tabloid-format newsletter directed to sales managers. Over the years the tabloid grew in subscriptions, size, and frequency. The name changed to *Selling Power*, and in magazine format it became the leader in the professional sales field. Every year *Selling Power* publishes the "Selling Power 500," a listing of the 500 largest sales forces in America. The company publishes books, sales training posters, and audio and video products for the professional sales market.

Gerhard has become America's leading expert on selling and sales management. He conducts webinars for such companies as SAP, and *Selling Power* has recently launched a new conference division that sponsors and conducts by-invitation-only leadership conferences directed toward companies with high sales volume and large sales forces.

For more information on *Selling Power* and its products and services, please visit www.sellingpower.com.

Maximum Impact

Everything I Know About Sales Success
THE WORLD'S GREATEST BUSINESS MINDS REVEAL THEIR WINNING SECRETS
Gerhard Gschwandtner
Founder and Publisher of Selling Power

201 Super Sales Tips
FIELD-TESTED STRATEGIES FOR PAINLESS PROSPECTING, PERFECT PRESENTATIONS, AND A QUICK CLOSE EVERY TIME
Gerhard Gschwandtner
Founder and Publisher of Selling Power

The Sales Closing Book
FIELD-TESTED CLOSES FOR EVERY SELLING SITUATION
Gerhard Gschwandtner
Founder and Publisher of Selling Power
Includes CD-ROM with Closings You Can Customize

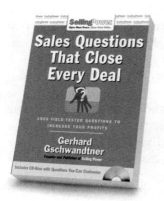
Sales Questions That Close Every Deal
1000 FIELD-TESTED QUESTIONS TO INCREASE YOUR PROFITS
Gerhard Gschwandtner
Founder and Publisher of Selling Power
Includes CD-Rom with Questions You Can Customize

Sales Scripts That Close Every Deal
420 TESTED RESPONSES TO 30 OF THE MOST DIFFICULT CUSTOMER OBJECTIONS
Gerhard Gschwandtner
Selling Power
Includes CD-Rom with Scripts You Can Customize

Mastering the Essentials of Sales
WHAT YOU NEED TO KNOW TO CLOSE EVERY SALE
Gerhard Gschwandtner
Founder and Publisher of Selling Power

ALSO AVAILABLE IN THE SELLING POWER LIBRARY

Great Thoughts to Sell By • The Psychology of Sales Success • Be In It to Win

Sales Stories to Sell By • Secrets of Superstar Sales Pros

Subscribe to *Selling Power* today and close more sales tomorrow!

GET 10 ISSUES – INCLUDING THE SALES MANAGER'S SOURCE BOOK.

In every issue of *Selling Power* magazine you'll find:

■ **A Sales Manager's Training Guide** with a one-hour sales training workshop complete with exercises and step-by-step instructions. Get a new guide in every issue! Created by proven industry experts who get $10,000 or more for a keynote speech or a training session.

■ **Best-practices reports** that show you how to win in today's tough market. Valuable tips and techniques for opening more doors and closing more sales.

■ **How-to stories** that help you speed up your sales cycle with innovative technology solutions, so you'll stay on the leading edge and avoid the "bleeding edge."

■ **Tested motivation ideas** so you and your team can remain focused, stay enthusiastic and prevail in the face of adversity.

Plus, you can sign up for five online SellingPower.com newsletters absolutely FREE.